DREAMING IN DARK TIMES

Dreaming in Dark Times

. . . .

Six Exercises in Political Thought

Sharon Sliwinski

University of Minnesota Press
Minneapolis
London

Chapter 1 was published in the Forerunners series of the University of Minnesota Press as *Mandela's Dark Years: A Political Theory of Dreaming* (2015).

A different version of chapter 2 was published as "The Freedom of Thought, in Dream-life if Nowhere Else: Freud, Foucault, and Euripides," *American Imago* 71, no. 3 (2014): 229–51. A different version of chapter 4 was published as "Air War and Dream: Photographing the London Blitz," *American Imago* 68, no. 3 (2011): 489–516.

Excerpt from *Hippolytus Temporizes & Ion* by H.D. (Hilda Doolittle) copyright 1927, 1937, by Hilda Aldington; copyright 1985, 1986, by Perdita Schaffner. Reprinted by permission of New Directions.

Excerpt from "Dulce et Decorum Est," by Wilfred Owen, is from Wilfred Owen, *The Complete Poems and Fragments*, edited by Jon Stallworthy (London: Chatto and Windus, 2013).

Published by the University of Minnesota Press
111 Third Avenue South, Suite 290
Minneapolis, MN 55401-2520
http://www.upress.umn.edu

A Cataloging-in-Publication record for this book
is available from the Library of Congress.
ISBN: 978-1-5179-0042-7 (hc)
ISBN: 978-1-5179-0043-4 (pb)

Printed in the United States of America on acid-free paper

The University of Minnesota is an equal-opportunity educator and employer.

24 23 22 21 20 19 18 17   10 9 8 7 6 5 4 3 2 1

Do they matter?—those dreams from the pit?

—Siegfried Sassoon, "Does It Matter?"

Excising the political from the life of the mind is a sacrifice that has proven costly.

—Toni Morrison, *Playing in the Dark*

Contents

A Fairy for an Introduction

ROMEO: *I dreamt a dream tonight.*
MERCUTIO: *And so did I.*
ROMEO: *Well, what was yours?*
MERCUTIO: *That dreamers often lie.*
ROMEO: *In bed asleep while they do dream things true.*
MERCUTIO: *O, then I see Queen Mab hath been with you.*

—Shakespeare, *Romeo and Juliet*

WHEN I BEGAN WRITING this book in earnest, I was beset by a particularly virulent case of wanderlust. I suspect the affliction is fairly common among writers, especially those facing a deadline. After several unrelenting weeks, I made my way to Sissinghurst Castle in the Weald of Kent, the one-time home of the English writer Vita Sackville-West. Vita's account of her own struggles with the condition had provided comfort, and a visit to her elaborate gardens, now kept by the British National Trust, somehow seemed to promise a cure.

The gardens and the surrounding grounds were extraordinary, but it was the trip home that provided the unexpected physic. When it came time to leave, I called a taxi to take me back to the train station. After the standard exchange, my affable driver asked me to speak to him a little, as he put it, "so I can guess where you're from." I obliged him by reporting that I was trying to write a book about dream-life and had been thinking about Queen Mab. He considered this for a moment and then burst into a rousing performance of the scene in question from *Romeo and Juliet*. I laughed and clapped, amazed by his familiarity with the play. He nodded his head in a little mock bow, but then, just as suddenly, grew crestfallen. Some moments passed between us in silence. He looked at me measuringly before disclosing his thoughts: "I haven't always been a taxi driver, you know. I'm an inventor, but I lost all my money." Then he told me a dream that had been troubling him for some time.

In the dream, this inventor-cum-taxi-driver found himself wandering around a small town, inexplicably forced to haul an elaborate cart wherever he went. The dream started off pleasantly enough: he smoked languorously and felt himself drawn to a little house that seemed familiar. But when he approached the owner—a kindly, beautiful matron—he was immediately set upon by a cruel bald man who growled menacingly at him: "Your kind isn't welcome here!" The dreamer fled but soon realized that he had left his cart in his hasty flight. The dream ended when he returned to the house to retrieve his transport, whereupon the bald man reappeared to reprimand him again. This time the dreamer calmly strangled his assailant to death.

The man was deeply perturbed by his dream and was full of genuine remorse for his imaginary act of murder. He was particularly troubled by his curious lack of feeling as he wrapped his fingers around the bald man's throat. "What do you think it means?" he asked me earnestly. I turned the question back to him and we began a long conversation about his life. He spoke of his inventions and dashed hopes, his great love of smoking and of women, his bond with his children, and his anguished relationship to his own father. I was sorry the ride was not longer. When we parted we shook hands as friends and he remembered that our conversation had begun with the fairy queen: "What a queer little creature," he mused wistfully as he helped me carry my bags up to the train platform.

Queen Mab's debut occurs in one of the more delirious speeches to have emerged from William Shakespeare's pen. Early in *Romeo and Juliet*, Mercutio tells the tale of this tiny fairy as a way to distract Romeo from his spurned love. Perhaps it is this proximity to mad passion that makes the character so compelling. In Mercutio's account, the fairy queen delivers her dreams while being carried through the air in a tiny carriage made out of a hazelnut shell (crafted either by a carpenter squirrel or an old grub worm). Mab's driver—a gray-coated gnat—takes his mistress to visit lovers, courtiers, lawyers, and soldiers. Galloping into lovers' brains, the fairy fills their thoughts with passionate embraces. When her carriage rides across sleeping courtiers' knees, they dream of perfect curtsies. When Mab visits lawyers, their fingers start grasping at fat imaginary fees. And when she spirits over a slumbering soldier's neck, he dreams of cutting foreign throats.

Queen Mab is the late sixteenth-century version of the dream-dealer. Like so many of these figures, Mab is something of a trickster. Just as often as she might decide to fulfill the dreamer's deepest desire, she might send terrible thoughts to wake them in a fright. Or she might refuse to come at all. She is a cruel and inconstant sprite—or so Mercutio claims. His speech has just begun to spiral into a dark place when Romeo interrupts his friend's frenzied ramblings: "Peace, peace, Mercutio, peace! Thou talk'st of nothing." Ever capricious, Mercutio shifts his tone again, responding to Romeo's intervention with one of the most breathtaking descriptions of oneiric-life ever put to paper:

> True, I talk of dreams,
> Which are the children of an idle brain,
> Begot of nothing but vain fantasy,
> Which is as thin of substance as the air
> And more inconstant than the wind.[1]

The strange, gossamer thoughts that come to us under the cover of sleep are all too quick to evaporate into the night. But then again, perhaps this is for the best—especially when the fairy queen delivers a nightmare so frightening that it becomes a relief to awaken.

One of the most compelling things about the figure of Queen Mab is the idea that dreams are delivered to us from someone and somewhere else. While these experiences seem to occur in the private theater of the mind, with the dreamer as the primary protagonist and sole spectator, in Shakespeare's version, we have little control over the production process. Queen Mab is a bit like an auteur director and we are her helpless audience, subject to her mercurial moods and unpredictable delivery schedule. In this respect, Shakespeare's character vividly illustrates one of the more distinctive features of dream-life: one can feel strangely vulnerable to these experiences, even if they are products of our own design. One is simultaneously the *subject of* dream-life and *subjected to* this uncanny world. Or put slightly differently, dreaming is among our most intimate encounters with the experience of being governed by an agency other than the self. And as my taxi driver remarked, it can be deeply disquieting to be treated like a foreigner in the landscape of one's own mind.

As a gesture of respect to your patience, let me tip my hand: in this book dream-life is treated neither as oracle nor as immanence. Building on Sigmund Freud's pioneering work, and drawing from a wide range of writers and thinkers since Freud's time, the central idea proposed here is that dreaming is a distinct species of thinking that can represent, contain, and transfigure the most profound of human conflicts. This particular form of thought involves a complex negotiation between one's inner objects and the remains of the day—a negotiation that often demands to be returned to the world through the dreamer's compulsive reporting of her dream. In narrating these thought-events, moreover, a dream becomes a particular kind of communication, a gossamer transport for the expression of difficult desires, ideas, and conflicts. This book pursues the idea that the various ways in which we negotiate these experiences can have profound significance for our social and political life together. Dreams are vehicles for otherwise unthinkable thoughts and a species of psychological work that can fold and transfigure the force of a harsh reality.

In short, this book defends the idea that *dream-life matters,* that attending to this thought-landscape is vital not only to the life of the individual but also to our shared social and political worlds.

Disclosing "It"

A few words about the structure of the argument. Like Queen Mab's roster of clients, this book has an ensemble cast. Each of the chapters works with a dream that has been plucked from the historical record, circling around this peculiar utterance to the milieu of its gestation. As I alluded to earlier in this introduction, there is a double wager involved in this method. The first part concerns the idea that these oneiric events can be understood as containing information that exceeds the dimension of the singular subject. Biography and history merge here. The reader will encounter the very private patterns of language and thought that structure individual memory, but these mental events are also taken as evidence that testifies to the conflicts of an era, as unconscious social knowledge conveyed in an alienated form. The British psychoanalyst Christopher Bollas named this unconscious material the "unthought known."[2] This is material that is either emotionally undigested or actively barred from consciousness. Dreams are attempts to represent and contain this material that each subject carries but that remains vexingly other. In this book, I am primarily interested in the social and political aspects of the unthought known. To adapt a pithy phrase from the American film critic Manny Farber, every dream transmits the DNA of its time. Attending to this unconscious material can offer access to the things that hover at the edge of our political imaginaries—the conflicts that preoccupy a particular cultural milieu, but which remain latent in its public discourse.

The second part of my wager involves the question of communication. At some point, each one of us has probably felt the powerful urge to share a dream with another person. The most common way to transmit this experience is to relay it through linguistic means. Freud often described the reporting of a dream as an "unconscious communication" or "utterance."[3] However, as anyone who has attempted to share a dream knows, this is an undoubtedly strange kind of speech, one we are not exactly the authors of. There is a fundamental distinction between the dream-as-dreamt and the dream-as-text, that is, from the actual experience of dreaming and the presentation of this experience in language afterward. These are two discrete activities that take place in two different moments. This book is concerned with both—with the complex mental activity called dreaming and also with the act of disclosing this experience to another person. Dreams have a way of compelling us to speak, and it is this latter gesture—the drive to disclose the experience to someone—that transforms dream-life into a political matter proper. Undoubtedly, narrating a dream represents a rather unusual mode of communication, but as the reader will see in the chapters that follow, such disclosures can serve as a potent form of political intervention—and perhaps especially, as Hannah Arendt would say, in those moments "when the chips are down."[4]

This latter aspect of my argument leans, in part, on Arendt's definition of politics. One of the preeminent political theorists of the late twentieth century, Arendt refused to define this field narrowly, as merely a matter of the power games played out between rulers and the ruled. For Arendt, politics takes place at the ground level of human affairs: in conversations with strangers and friends, in the actions and appearances we make in public, indeed, in any activity that involves the exercise of freedom. For Arendt, freedom is the raison d'être of politics, and its field of expression is speech and action. As she once put it, freedom and politics are related to each other "like two sides of the same matter."[5] Speaking and acting with a view to freedom are the principal means by which human beings disclose themselves to the world and thereby renew the polis—the shared political world that lies between us.

Arendt herself did not write about dream-life (although she did support one of her friends in this very endeavor, as I discuss in chapter 6). In fact, in her most celebrated book, *The Human Condition*, Arendt drew a sharp distinction between the public and private realms. Nevertheless, I think we can borrow and adapt her definition of politics for our purposes, not least because the political theorist herself turned her attention to the life of the mind at the end of her career.

Arendt defined the political sphere as a symbolic environment fashioned from the vast web of human relations, and more precisely, from the particular activity of individuals disclosing themselves to one another: "With word and deed we insert ourselves into the human world," she proposed, "and this insertion is like a second birth, in which we confirm and take upon ourselves the naked fact of our original physical appearance."[6] In *The Human Condition*, Arendt distinguished this particular activity of disclosing oneself from both work and labor. Inserting ourselves into the political realm is not forced upon us by necessity, nor prompted by utility: "Its impulse springs from the beginning which came into the world when we were born and to which we respond by beginning something new on our own initiative."[7]

My encounter with the taxi driver at Sissinghurst Castle makes Arendt's distinction plainly evident: it was not through his labor or his work that this man conveyed his uniqueness to me, but rather in the risk he took to speak to a stranger in a way that involved the courage of truth. Both the content and his manner of speaking revealed his sincerity as a speaker. In narrating his dream, he disclosed something specific about his lived experience. This peculiar narrative aimed to provide an account of *who* he was, apart from *what* he was (namely, a taxi driver).

Admittedly, reporting a dream is a rather unusual method of inserting oneself into the public realm, not least because these strange speech acts operate without mastery of their content. This particular communicative action is not governed by reason. In this respect, I am working some distance from the common definition of the public sphere as an arena of rational argumentation.[8] Reporting a dream involves the disclosure of a rather different kind of information. Indeed, despite the sincerity of his narrative, my taxi driver found it difficult to say exactly *what* his dream was about, or indeed, *who* had authored the strange narrative that he found himself reporting to me. Nevertheless, I understood his disclosure to be a significant means for him to convey something about his lived experience— something he could not express otherwise. To borrow the American novelist Toni Morrison's powerful phrase, his dream provided the vehicle to articulate "unspeakable things unspoken."[9]

Arendt privileged storytelling in her theory of political action. She prominently cited the Danish novelist Isak Dinesen in *The Human Condition*:

"All sorrows can be borne if you put them into a story or tell a story about them."[10] The gesture of giving voice to our disparate experiences, Arendt argued, creates a vital bridge between the public and private realms. In her view, storytelling is a means whereby personal experiences and shared perspectives can be interwoven and reworked in the company of others—a purposeful action (or praxis) that discloses our uniqueness, our connection to others, and the environmental forces to which we are subject.[11] Of course, these environmental conditions affect different members of the polis in different ways. All social polities are riven by competing discourses. Although Arendt did not emphasize it, the politics of storytelling also concerns *which* stories are recognized as legitimate and, conversely, which voices are barred from being heard in the public realm. Arendt came to the United States as a refugee and spent almost ten years as a stateless person. While she emphasized the power of storytelling to connect us with others, she also intuitively grasped and advocated for the position of "conscious pariah"—the voice of the outlander who stands on the border of society and who can reflect on the vested interests of power from this distance. Morrison herself has offered a related strategy for interrogating those political environments that solicit stories from some members of the political community while, at the same time, actively work to disenfranchise and silence others.

In *Dreaming in Dark Times*, I am principally interested in the stories we have trouble telling, the things we struggle to voice—even to ourselves. When we cannot consciously formulate a story, the experience often demands another venue of expression: through dreams, symptoms, or other unconscious actions. There is an urgent need to find ways to incorporate this disavowed material into our shared political imaginaries—to identify and integrate the unspeakable things unspoken. Or in Jacqueline Rose's words, we need to find a political language that can "confront the subterranean aspects of history and the human mind, both of which play their part in driving the world on its course, but which our dominant political vocabularies most often cannot bear to face."[12] This book does not so much seek a new language as revive an old method for engaging this unconscious material, namely, by returning to one of the original access points that Freud identified—dream-life.

Today few people believe that a fairy queen delivers our dreams. We are perhaps more likely to say, "*It* came to me in a dream," which is one way to signal that the experience feels like it has arrived from elsewhere.

Dreaming is an intimate brush with a particular kind of otherness that inhabits each of us. "It" is also a common way to refer to the unconscious—what Sigmund Freud described in German as *das Es* (literally, "It").[13] In psychoanalytic terms, dreaming represents a complex dialogue with the unconscious. A word of caution is perhaps in order here. Although it might be obvious, given the absurdity that can reign in the landscape of dream-life, the reader should keep in mind that the unconscious is not organized by the same laws of mental functioning as the more conscious levels of thought. Unconscious modes of thought and feeling are only grasped with difficulty owing, in part, to the force of repression (this is one reason why dreams are so easily "forgotten").

Tarrying with "It" means, therefore, tarrying with the ways one is necessarily subjected to laws beyond the self. Dream-life is one of the more intimate venues where this struggle for sovereignty over the self plays out. We are not in command of our dream plots. Narrating these experiences, by extension, represents a kind of speech act that divests the speaker of his or her authorial agency. Or to borrow Sarah Kofman's more elegant phrasing, relaying a dream is a kind of speaking *sans pouvoir*—a kind of speaking *without power*.[14] In my mind, this makes dream-life a particularly fertile site for thinking about the schisms of subjectivity and agency, but also for grappling with the dilemmas of sovereignty. Dreams can arouse unsettling questions about desire and self-governance. These experiences provide proof, as Freud put it, that we are not the masters of our own house. Part of the wager of this book rests on the idea that the struggles occurring in the arena of dream-life can provide insight into larger questions of political governance. Indeed, as many of the dreamers in this book show, speaking of one's oneiric life can serve as a particularly potent strategy for negotiating and resisting certain forms of sovereign power—a means to unsettle the power–knowledge relations of a given era.

As my terminology suggests, the other guiding inspiration for this project is the French philosopher Michel Foucault. Foucault did not characterize himself as a political theorist, but he was committed to finding new and more effective ways of political seeing. Like Arendt, Foucault understood political power to be a matter of how the private realm of individual experience connects to the public realm. The question of speech was important to both thinkers. In his last years, Foucault began studying the genealogy of various forms of truth-telling in the political realm and he became particularly interested in what the ancient Greeks called *parrhēsia,* a term that is often translated as "free speech," although Foucault conducted an extended genealogy of the word.[15]

For most of his career, the philosopher had been preoccupied with processes of domination, and more pointedly, with institutional mechanisms that transform subjects into objects: "the divisions operating in society in the name of madness, disease, delinquency and their effects on the formation of a reasonable and normal subject."[16] But Foucault came to realize that he had neglected the critical techniques by which one constitutes *oneself* as a subject—the various practices by which one can establish a relationship to oneself. This new line of research still fell within the purview of his overarching concerns about power–knowledge relations, but it was also a means to open up new possibilities and questions about human agency. As Foucault discussed in his last book, *The Care of the Self,* dream interpretation was one of the common "techniques of self" in the ancient world. For the ancients, disclosing a dream to another person was one of the established means to decipher, examine, and avow the truth about one's desire in relation to the particular conditions of one's social existence.[17] Dreams manifest our unique bond to the social imaginary.

Today, it is relatively rare to turn to dream-life as a site to interrogate one's place in the world. Modernity seems to have sapped all significance from oneiric-life. But this has not stopped people from dreaming. Nor has it stopped people from disclosing their dreams to one another as a way of inserting themselves into the human world. Perhaps it is time to turn our attention to these unconscious communications, to listen more closely to what is being expressed in these diaries of the night.

Thinking in the Dark

The following chapters examine a handful of dreams drawn from the annals of the twentieth century. Each of these avowals is treated as an unconventional species of political thought. The catchphrase of the project, if I can put it that way, is borrowed from Freud, who regularly argued that dreams are simply a "particular *form* of thought" made possible by the condition of sleep.[18] Dreams *think,* Freud insisted, although this unconscious form of thought bears little resemblance to more familiar modes of conscious reasoning. Dream-thinking restages our conflicts in the theater of the mind, transfiguring painful experiences—actually re-presenting them a new guise—so as to shield us from their impact. This psychological labor aims to protect us from the slings and arrows of life, and simultaneously, to emotionally digest these events in ways that keep us alive to life.

The dreams under examination here are somewhat atypical. Of course not all dream-life is destined to become a political matter. Since ancient times, dream interpreters have identified various types of dreams. In his second-century, five-volume work *Oneirocritica,* for instance, Artemidorus distinguished between the dreams that concern bodily states and the dreams that refer to events in the world. In his own *Interpretation of Dreams,* written two millennia later, Freud listed three kinds of "typical dreams": exhibition dreams, dreams of the death of a loved one, and examination dreams. Dream-life, like so much of waking-life, is preoccupied with finding a means to represent our physical and mental states. But social and political matters also weigh on the mind, creating conflicts that demand to be represented and worked through, even in our sleep.

My aim here is not so much to carve out a separate taxonomy of political dreams but rather to grasp how the transmission of this unconscious form of knowledge operates during what Hannah Arendt described as dark times. Dark times are turbulent political moments in which the public realm has been infected with a kind of black light. Arendt lived through the Nazis' rise to power in Germany, but she did not only have the Third Reich in mind. Dark times, she suggests, do not just appear with totalitarian regimes. Rather, she marked these eras by a certain kind of suppression of speech and public declaration, and simultaneously, by an all-too-public display of evildoing. In dark times, social and political violence is both overtly visible and yet oddly difficult to recognize.[19]

In one of her least celebrated books, *Men in Dark Times,* Arendt drew attention to the way language works—or rather how it *fails* to work—in such climates. She noticed that human speech becomes divested of its power to represent and transmit the truth during these periods. A kind of perverse language emerges instead that tends to serve those who wish to prolong the distorted political situation. Arendt specifically mentions "the highly efficient double-talk" of official representatives who invent many ingenious ways to "explain away unpleasant facts."[20] This kind of language is designed to obfuscate reality, thwarting the citizenry's capacity for thought. Stock phrases and standardized codes of expression start to become pervasive. As the Israeli novelist David Grossman memorably describes, the language of the citizenry who live through prolonged political conflict "becomes flatter and flatter as the conflict goes on, gradually evolving into a series of clichés and slogans."[21]

This book aims to show how dream-life can serve to reanimate a world that has been flattened by dark times. Dreams are a crucial resource for regaining a measure of freedom in our thought and speech, serving as a vital landscape to recover our fundamental human capacity to assign meaning to the world. Dreaming is a wellspring in this respect, albeit one that works somewhat akin to the ancient oracles: the information that dreams provide requires a significant amount of psychological labor to decipher. And sometimes these experiences can feel like a cruel diktat—especially when one is tormented by nightmares. But this is ultimately a life-preserving activity. When linked to waking-thought, dreaming plays an important role in feeling alive. Dreams animate human life; that is their work.

The dreamers you will meet in these pages are in their own ways grappling with their dream-life as a means to conjure up the courage to speak about their experience of dark times. The landscapes are dramatically varied, as are the conditions of the disclosure of the dream: a notorious prison from apartheid-era South Africa (in chapter 1); the tangle of sexual relations in fin de siècle Vienna (in chapter 2); an Allied military hospital during the Great War (in chapter 3); one of the longest city sieges in history, the London Blitz (in chapter 4); the psychiatric wards of colonial Algeria (in chapter 5); and Berlin under the Third Reich (in chapter 6). While the climate conditions in each of these cases are unique, in each instance I treat the reported dream as an extraordinarily fragile means by which an individual sought to disclose something about the terms of his or her existence—a means to exercise a measure of freedom despite the pressures of the time.

A Note on Technique

The reader deserves a few words about methodology. Freud himself was profoundly skeptical about working with dreams from the historical record. When he replied to a letter from an admirer who was attempting to analyze several of Descartes's dreams, he didn't mince words: "Working on dreams without being able to obtain from the dreamer himself any indications on the relations which might link them to one another or attach them to the external world . . . gives, as a general rule, only a meagre result."[22]

From a psychoanalytic vantage, the dreamer's associations to his or her dream are a vital and necessary part of the process of interpretation. These associations include all the networks of ideas, stray thoughts, and seemingly random images that come to mind in relation to the manifest content of the dream. My taxi driver readily offered up his own associations to the contents of his dream in the course of our conversation. Without this material, dreams are mute artifacts, and any attempt to conduct an interpretation is perilously proximate to "wild" analysis.[23] Interpretation must flow from the dreamer; it is considered an injustice to impose meaning on these experiences from on high, so to speak.

As the psychoanalyst Ella Freeman Sharpe once described, a dream is an individual psychic product derived from a storehouse of specific lived experiences.[24] One needs an intimate knowledge of the person whose dreams are subject to interpretation, as well as an understanding of the cultural environment of its gestation. As you might imagine, this requirement posed a significant methodological dilemma. I had discovered a number of fascinating dream-reports in the historical record, but there were few accounts of the dreamer's associations to this material. As evocative as these objects were, they remained mute. To adapt one of Walter Benjamin's aphorisms: a dream-report is rather like the death mask of the dream's conception.[25] For a time, I was at a loss about what to do with these strange artifacts. The road seemed blocked.

A solution presented itself in the form of a lecture given by Adrian Kohler and Basil Jones, the two founders of the Handspring Puppet Company. (The solution is not obvious; you will have to bear with me for a moment.) In the lecture, the puppeteers spoke eloquently about their artistic process, recounting an early collaboration with the artist William Kentridge on an opera called *Il ritorno d'Ulisse* (The return of Ulysses). The staging of the production called for a puppet version of Ulysses to lie inert in a hospital bed while his thoughts and dreams were conveyed to the audience via the opera singers. At first the puppeteers were baffled about how to marry these two very different kinds of performers: puppets and singers. It didn't help that they didn't have a shared a language between them—the opera was in Italian and the puppeteers are South African.

Kohler and Jones studied the singers for a while and eventually seized upon a small detail: they noticed that before singing a single note, each singer took a quick inhalation. This relatively simple observation catalyzed an important recognition. They realized that to make the two sets of performers operate in the same emotional universe, the puppets also had to breathe. The result was startling. Audiences were completely mesmerized by the tiny breaths of the sleeping, dreaming puppet lying inert in a hospital bed, movements that were sometimes as little as five millimeters in amplitude, but which spectators seemed to register even at the back of the auditorium.

At the time, the puppeteers have admitted, they didn't quite know what was happening, but the experience made them realize the primacy of breath in their practice. As an inanimate performer, a puppet has a rather unusual ontological status: it must *strive to live*.[26] Breath is the original movement in this drama, the primary gesture in the overall emotional engineering of their artistic practice.

As anyone who has spent time with someone who is on the threshold of life knows, breath can be *the* decisive indicator of life. In the case of the theater performance, members of the audience understand they are observing an illusion. The puppeteers make no attempt to hide their manipulations; in fact, the puppet operators are always visible participants in Handspring Company's performances. But somehow this transparency does not cancel the perilous thrill of witnessing the puppet's striving for life. Indeed, precisely because of the visibility of the illusion, the spectator feels called upon to add her seal of verification, to give over her critical faculty as an integral part of the overall emotional effect of the performance. This has nothing to do with being an enlightened or knowledgeable spectator, but rather turns on the sense of being intimately involved in the performance. One feels keenly aware of being an integral participant in this dramatic struggle for meaning, indeed, *for life*. As Kentridge remarks, "It's about the *unwilling* suspension of disbelief. In spite of knowing that the puppet is a piece of wood operated by an actor, you find yourself ascribing agency to it."[27]

In my own way, I have borrowed and adapted the puppeteers' artistic practice as a methodological technique. Here dreaming is understood as an intersubjective event that requires animation—a special orchestration of voice and breath.[28] Like the puppets, dreams possess a queer kind of agency that outstrips our conscious control. Even when the dreamer is alive to anchor them in a lived reality, these oneiric events can be experienced as uncanny, which is to say, dreams separate the dreamer from the restrictions of reality and initiate an engagement with unconscious material.[29] In less technical terms, dreams are peopled by mysterious doubles of friends, family, lovers, and strangers—both living and dead. The landscape of dream-life has its own particular set of environmental conditions that can feel simultaneously familiar *and* strange, threatening *and* comforting.

Keeping this uncanny texture in mind, the following chapters try to set the stage in a way so that each of the dreams under scrutiny might be given room to breathe. There is a necessarily performative aspect to each of these narratives. Rather than attempt to interpret the dreams, I have aimed to construct a situation in which the utterance could be encountered anew so that readers could wonder at this strange disclosure. Like the puppeteers, I have vivified what is an otherwise inanimate object. Treating dreams this way—as performative statements that require animation, as "writerly" scripts in Roland Barthes's terms—seems infinitely more fruitful than quibbling over a "correct" interpretation.[30] I invite you to lend your ear and your imagination to this process, to allow these unconscious testimonies to resonate—testimonies that, when they are recorded at all, are usually only heard sotto voce, like a whisper in the night.

The overarching gamble of this book is to dare to treat dream-life as though one might find wisdom, courage, and freedom in this alternative thought-landscape. I leave it to the reader to decide if the wager has been a good one.

The Prisoner's Defense

The Ghost House Dream

ONE GRAY DAY not so long ago, I found myself wandering around an airport bookstore. I suspect you are familiar with the kind of place; it was one of those brightly lit kiosks with tiered banks of magazines and pocket-sized paperbacks that are designed to capture the attention of the jet-lagged traveler. I browsed for a while and was about to leave empty handed when Nelson Mandela's smiling face caught my eye. I had wanted to read his autobiography, *Long Walk to Freedom,* for some time, and when the venerable leader died at the end of 2013, the desire was revived. I purchased the hefty volume and headed off to my departure gate.

Mandela's autobiography begins, predictably enough, with the story of his childhood. Places and names are significant to his narrative. Born to the Thembu royal family, he was given the Xhosa forename Rolihlahla at his birth (which colloquially means "troublemaker"). When he was sent away to school at age seven, he acquired a clan name, Madiba (which continues to be used as a sign of respect and affection), a patrilineal grandfather provided his surname, and his first teacher, in accordance with colonial custom, gave him a Christian name, Nelson. After a rebellious youth, Mandela eventually made his way to the University of the Witwatersrand, where he slowly worked toward a degree (repeatedly failing his qualifying exams) as the only black law student.

You probably know the basic outlines of what happened next: as a young lawyer practicing in Johannesburg in the 1940s, he joined the African National Congress Party. In 1951, after the National Party took power, he helped organize the Defiance Campaign in response to the new apartheid laws. When the ANC's nonviolent tactics were met with violent reprisals from the Afrikaner government, Mandela began advocating for a different strategy. In 1961 he publicly stated, "If the government reaction is to crush by naked force our non-violent struggle, we will have to reconsider our tactics."[1] The young leader suffered a series of bans, served several jail sentences, and eventually cofounded the militant wing of the ANC, Umkhonto we Sizwe (or MK). He went underground and undertook guerrilla warfare training, but was eventually captured and tried at the infamous Rivonia Trial, in which he and seven other ANC members were found guilty of a series of charges related to sabotage. Narrowly escaping the death penalty, Mandela was sentenced to life in prison on June 12, 1964. He did not see freedom again until February 11, 1990. After his release, he went on to lead the transitional government and became the first democratically elected president of South Africa, serving just one term, from 1994 to 1999.

What enthralled me most about the autobiography was the section called "The Dark Years." The title refers to the years Mandela spent imprisoned on Robben Island. This part of the book reads like a training manual for surviving dark times. Madiba describes the various hardships imposed at the newly designed prison: a discriminatory dress code and segregated diet that the government created for each of the four racial groups it had invented ("black," "white," "coloured," and "Indian"), brutal forced labor at the island's lime quarry, and harsh restrictions on visitors and letters (one visitor and one letter were permitted every six months, always censored and often denied altogether). There is a sparse account of Mandela's devastation at the news of his mother's death in 1968. This grief was deepened less than a year later when he received a telegram informing him of his eldest son's death as a result of injuries sustained in a car crash. Each of these experiences imposed a distinct psychological pressure: "The challenge for every prisoner, particularly every political prisoner," Mandela counsels, "is how to survive prison intact, how to emerge from prison undiminished, how to conserve and even replenish one's beliefs."[2]

It was not, however, these soul-rending accounts or the leader's startling capacity for perseverance that brought me up short on that long flight. What jolted me awake was, in fact, a dream. Or to be more precise, a nightmare, which Mandela reports returned repeatedly to haunt him during his twenty-seven-year imprisonment:

> I had one recurring nightmare. In the dream, I had just been
> released from prison—only it was not Robben Island, but a jail in
> Johannesburg. I walked outside the gates into the city and found
> no one there to meet me. In fact, there was no one there at all, no
> people, no cars, no taxis. I would then set out on foot toward

Soweto. I walked for many hours before arriving in Orlando West, and then turned the corner toward 8115. Finally, I would see my home, but it turned out to be empty, a ghost house, with all the doors and windows open, but no one at all there.[3]

I can still remember my sense of astonishment in coming across this passage. It was the middle of the night and I was cramped, reading by that single, sharp light that beams down from the bulkhead. I felt seized by a powerful urge to wake the passenger next to me so I could share the moment with someone. Mandela's nightmare seemed just as dramatic and important as his famous speech from the Rivonia Trial in which he named apartheid's injustice and defined the ideal for which he was prepared to die: a democratic and free society.[4] His nightmare seemed to attest to something similarly poignant about his experience of prison, offering both a private account of his emotional state and a profound testimony about the political conditions of his unfreedom.

But then came the questions: Exactly what kind of statement was this? What does a dream manage to say—or rather *to show*—that is not legible otherwise? Indeed, what does *this* recurring dream manage to show of Mandela's experience of prison? Can this disclosure be understood as a form of political avowal? To what, exactly, does a dream attest? And to whom?

Dream-Thinking

As Sigmund Freud proposed, dreaming is a distinct species of thinking. He wrote voluminously on the subject, but offered one of his clearest statements on the matter in a footnote added to *The Interpretation of Dreams* in 1925: "At bottom, dreams are nothing more than particular *form* of thinking made possible by the condition of the state of sleep."[5] I take this statement to be axiomatic. *Dreams think*, Freud insists, even as this psychological activity bears little affinity to the more familiar forms of conscious thought.

More precisely, Freud suggests that a dreamer *experiences* her thoughts rather than "thinks" them in concepts. Dreams dramatize an idea, constructing a situation out of thoughts that have been transposed onto images.[6] Moreover, while the particular scenes and actions of dream-life might seem utterly alien to waking-thought, they nevertheless arise out of incidents of our lived experience. Dream-life is anchored in the material world, tethered to the particular conflicts and conditions of the dreamer's social situation. These thought-events are a kind of mental *bricolage*, to borrow one of Claude Lévi-Strauss's terms, a particular form of thinking that reuses and recombines bits and pieces of material both from the dreamer's diurnal perceptions and the vast storehouse of memory traces.[7]

The various locations mentioned in Mandela's dream can certainly be traced back to sites of his lived experience: the jail in Johannesburg where he spent time awaiting trial in 1962 prior to the Rivonia Trial, but also the first home he owned, the little redbrick house, number 8115 in Orlando West, a place Mandela once called the "center point" of his world, "the place marked with an X in my mental geography."[8] This modest building has subsequently taken on another layer of significance since 1999 when it was rebuilt and transformed into a museum that now receives thousands of visitors each year. The nightmare also manages to index the tiny cell on Robben Island in which Mandela spent the majority of his sentence, albeit only through a negation: the dream-prison "was *not* Robben Island," he insists. Such cancellations are a telltale sign of repression, a signal that something is being withheld from consciousness because of the pain that would come with its acknowledgement.[9]

While dream-life relies on elements of the dreamer's storehouse of experience to weave its landscapes, this is undoubtedly a queer kind of thinking. These uncanny mental events share more than a passing affinity to Franz Kafka's breathtaking thought-landscapes: "When Gregor Samsa woke one morning from uneasy dreams, he found himself transformed into some kind of monstrous vermin."[10] The dream-landscape, like Kafka's stories, operates under an unusual set of environmental conditions. Dream-life is not a documentary presentation of events but rather a *symbolic* account of the dreamer's lived experience. In Mandela's case, his dream visually staged the sense of alienation and unfreedom that the prolonged incarceration inflicted: freedom to wander in an empty, uninhabited world is, of course, no freedom at all. Far from being a straightforward fantasy of escape, the nightmare achingly dramatized what a life separated from one's loved ones felt like for the dreamer. It also testified to the experience of being ostracized from the larger political community of humanity, *showing* what it means to be denied the primary dimension of the human condition that involves belonging to a shared gaze—*to see and to be seen to exist.*[11]

In Freud's time, just as now, the idea of treating dream-life as an object of study—as a particular *form* of thinking—was considered an outrageous leap. As Freud points out in the opening pages of his *Interpretation of*

Dreams, the perplexity this nocturnal phenomenon presented to scientific reasoning is so generally admitted in the literature that "it seems unnecessary to quote instances in support of it."[12] Freud's theory of interpretation posed a direct challenge to the logic of the sciences of his day (a challenge that remains just as potent today, in our own era, which is dominated by cognitive models of brain functioning). By insisting that these seemingly nonsensical psychological events contain meaning and, moreover, that their strange logic is a deliberate attempt to thwart rationality, Freud generated a powerful critique of Enlightenment reasoning.[13] In wrestling with the force of the unconscious, he dared to stray beyond the borders of rational thought and yet refused to jettison meaning from this territory. Or as Jacqueline Rose has more elegantly phrased it, "Psychoanalysis starts from the premise that we are freighted with a form of knowledge we cannot bear."[14] Dream-life is one of the key points of contact with this unconscious knowledge that each of us carries but does not quite possess.

Freud was not alone in his exploration of the territory that lies beyond the gates of rationality. In the later half of the twentieth century, a variety of political thinkers began to notice the cracks in the bedrock of reason that had once served as the privileged foundation of political thought. Some of these theorists diagnosed the Enlightenment itself as a disturbed form of thinking and began searching for alternatives. In the preface to her collection of essays titled *Between Past and Future,* Hannah Arendt offers a terse account of this landscape of postwar critique. Having barely escaped the Nazis' genocidal designs, Arendt knew all too well how political terror could be unleashed in the voice of reason. She notes that the French intellectuals who joined the *résistance* and who founded existentialism were not the first, nor the last, to have "outbursts of passionate exasperation with reason, thought, and rational discourse." Such are "the natural reactions of men who know from their own experiences that thought and reality have parted company."[15] But in her characteristically strong-minded way, Arendt dismissed existentialism as representing little more than a form of escapism—an attempt to evade the dilemmas of dark times by retreating into an "unquestioning commitment to action."[16] In her mind, becoming an *engagée* was no solution for the profound problems that arise when reason breaks with reality.

For the latter half of her life, Arendt searched for an elastic form of thinking that could endure the dilemmas of dark times. She wrote at length about the problem of "thoughtlessness" and yet she never gave up on the activity of thinking. The essays that make up *Between Past and Future* represent a series of such experiments in thinking otherwise. She subtitled the collection *Eight Exercises in Political Thought*. They are not prescriptions about *what* to think so much as experiments in *how* to think. Like many theorists of her generation, Arendt moved away from sweeping philosophical treatises and opted instead to examine aspects of our shared intellectual tradition from the standpoint of subjective experience. She advocated for a kind of thinking that arose out of the "actuality of political incidents." Her assumption was that "thought itself arises out of incidents of living experience and must remain bound to them as the only guideposts by which to take its bearings."[17]

Mandela can be taken as an exemplar of such thinking. Over and over, he demonstrated the kind of "enlarged thought" that the political theorist championed. Arendt borrowed this term from Immanuel Kant (she worked closely with the philosopher's theory of judgment in *Lectures on Kant's Political Philosophy*, published posthumously).[18] For both thinkers, "enlarged thought" is an exemplary mental process by which one imagines the world from the perspective of the other, or, as Kant articulated it, "to think from the standpoint of everyone else."[19] The philosopher situated this activity as one of the maxims for a common human understanding, and Arendt extended this line of thinking to argue that this specific mental process was integral to our collective political reality—an indispensible exercise of imagination that actually creates and sustains our common public world.

When the "hope of Africa" sprang through the prison's door in 1994, not only was his "stupendous heart" and "gargantuan will" intact but Mandela had also somehow managed to use his twenty-seven years of imprisonment to extend his capacity to think from the standpoint of others.[20] When he took the seat of presidency in a country in which he had previously not been allowed to vote, he personally—and courteously—invited his former prison guards to sit in the front rows of his inauguration. As Rita Barnard has argued, Mandela's approach to politics borrowed from the genre of the sublime, which is to say, his expansive understanding of freedom exceeded the confines of all the available models that traditionally give shape to this ideal.[21] South Africa's transition to democracy certainly cannot be attributed to one man—and Mandela's record is not without controversy—but there can be no doubt that his striking capacity to think from the standpoint of others had an integral part to play in the larger transformation of his country. Mandela's example underscores Arendt's fundamental insight: that the individual's ability *to think* has a profound relationship to the political commons.

Mandela himself provides a brief account of how he came to acquire this enlarged mentality in the closing paragraphs of his autobiography: "I was not born with a hunger to be free," he writes, although as a boy he felt free—free to run in the fields, swim in the streams, roast "mealies," and ride the broad backs of the bulls in his village. It was only as a young man that he began to understand his boyhood freedom was an illusion, and it was then that his gnawing hunger began. As a student, and then as a barrister in Johannesburg, he yearned for the freedom not to be obstructed in earning a living wage, to marry and raise a family, to live a lawful life. But he found that achieving these goals did not satisfy his hunger: "I saw that it was not just my freedom that was curtailed, but the freedom of everyone who looked like I did." Joining the ANC helped him understand that his hunger was indivisible from the freedom of his people to live with dignity: "The chains on any one of my people were the chains on all of them, the chains on all of my people were the chains on me."

Such narratives of disillusionment are familiar enough as the makings of a freedom fighter. But Mandela's thought had more maturing to do. The long and lonely years in prison transformed his hunger for his people's freedom into a hunger for the freedom of all people:

> I knew as well as I knew anything that the oppressor must be liberated just as surely as the oppressed. A man who takes away another man's freedom is a prisoner of hatred, he is locked behind the bars of prejudice and narrow-mindedness. . . . The oppressed and the oppressor alike are robbed of their humanity.
>
> When I walked out of prison, that was my mission, to liberate the oppressed and the oppressor both. Some say that has now been achieved. But I know that is not the case. The truth is that we are not yet free; we have merely achieved the freedom to be free, the right not to be oppressed. We have not taken the final step of our journey, but the first step on a longer and even more difficult road. For to be free is not merely to cast off one's chains, but to live in a way that respects and enhances the freedom of others.[22]

In these stirring closing passages, one can hear echoes of a universal humanism that stretches from the eighteenth-century revolutions through to the United Nations' Declaration of Human Rights, adopted in 1948. There are also deep reverberations that come from years of anticolonial struggle and the wellspring of *ubuntu*, an African-born philosophy that attends to the obligations of kinship and advocates a model of humanity-in-reciprocity: the profound sense that we are human only through the humanity of others. Mandela's ability to borrow from a startlingly wide range of political traditions makes him one of the exemplars of enlarged thought. He gave birth to an indivisible notion of freedom, which, aside from transforming him into a global icon for human rights, can serve as a model for Arendt's signature claim that "the *raison d'être* of politics is freedom."[23]

I am aware that I have taken us on a detour away from the particulars of Mandela's nightmare. The point of this diversion was not only to make a case for his significance as an exemplary political thinker of the twentieth century but also to show that some of the most potent and transformative forms of political thought do not depend on rationality. In dark times, another form of thinking is needed.

Mandela's dream bears the scars of such a climate. A recurring nightmare is a particular form of thinking that operates under the pressure of fear. The dreams that leave us crying out in the dark demand a special kind of psychological work. In Wilfred Bion's terms, these frightening mental events are the psyche's attempt to digest a particularly difficult emotional experience. The dream subjects the dreamer's emotional pain to a specific form of unconscious work that is designed to induce psychological growth.[24]

Put more simply, nightmares call for courage. And as Hannah Arendt noted, courage is cardinal among the political virtues.[25] This attribute is what enables and emboldens us to leave the protective confines of our homes and to enter the public realm. Mandela's example reminds us that courage does not come without its share of anguish. The recurring nightmare is one example of its psychic cost, but his autobiography is filled with descriptions of the excruciating divide he felt between the obligations of family life and the obligations of public life. (In the closing pages one can find the final wrenching account: "It was as simple and yet as incomprehensible as the moment when a small child asks her father, 'Why can you not be with us?' And the father must utter the terrible words, 'There are other children like you, a great many of them . . .' and then one's voice trails off.")[26] Mandela spent the better part of his lifetime digesting this difficult knowledge: in dark times, it is not only individual lives at stake but the larger human world.

From this fraught climate, the significance of dream-life can perhaps begin to stand out. To transpose Arendt's terms into a Freudian key: dreaming is an integral exercise of thought, an alternative landscape built out of incidents of living experience, and a prime model of our fundamental human capacity to assign meaning to the world. Without relying on the banisters of existent concepts, dream-thinking manages to dramatize and metabolize our most profound conflicts, geolocating the moorings of our subjectivity within the gossamer web of social relations, all without losing an inch in the riches, varieties, and dramatic elements that are so characteristic of "real" life.

The following sections elaborate this central premise, echoing and deepening the idea that dream-thinking is integral to the political realm. Each of the sections pursues an interrelated idea: (1) dream-work as a model of civil defense, (2) narrating a dream as a discourse that acts, and (3) dreaming as a practice of freedom. Various aspects of these ideas are also elaborated in the chapters that follow.

The guiding principle that animates these explorations is borrowed from the pediatrician and psychoanalyst D. W. Winnicott, who, at the close of World War II, offered this wise counsel: "Thinking is but a snare and a delusion unless the unconscious is taken into account."[27]

Dream-Work as Civil Defense

One of the things that makes dreams infinitely more adventurous, more inventive, and more cunning than daytime thought is the fact that this thought-landscape is not governed by the rules of rationality but rather relies on a alternative mode of mental functioning in which meaning moves more freely.

In chapter 7 of *The Interpretation of Dreams,* Freud named this particular form of thought "primary process." He juxtaposed this mode of thinking to "secondary process," under which he included the more familiar operations of waking thought—reasoning, attention, judgment, and so on. Freud's attempt to distinguish these two modes of thought helped him elucidate the dynamic operations of the unconscious. Dreaming is just one example of unconscious thinking, but it was through the extended examination of these oneiric events that Freud was able to elaborate the workings of this agency. Primary process thinking should not, therefore, be marked "irrational" against the presumed "rationality" of secondary processes. Primary process simply obeys a different set of laws—and dreams are paradigmatic of its "implicit logic."[28]

Central to this implicit logic is a distinction between two separate functions, both of which operate unconsciously in the formation of a dream: first, there is the production of the *dream-thoughts*. Second is the transformation of these thoughts into the manifest content of the dream through the operations of the *dream-work*.[29]

Dream-thoughts are the dense web of thoughts and ideas that are latent in a dream but that can be gradually unearthed through the dreamer's associations, that is, all the memories, thoughts, and images that each element of the dream brings to mind. For the first half of his career, Freud maintained that these dream-thoughts were arranged according to a pleasure principle, hence his oft-cited thesis that a dream is the fulfillment of a repressed wish. This led some analysts to assume that dreams could be distilled to a single desire, but Freud more often than not described dream-thoughts in terms of a dense thicket, as "a complex of thoughts and memories of the most intricate possible structure, with all the attributes of trains of thought familiar to us in waking life."[30]

For a time, Freud was preoccupied by these intricate "trains of thought," which, as he notes, can emerge from more than one center. But as his thinking matured, he realized that the more radical aspect of dream-life was not the unconscious thoughts themselves but the particular way these thoughts are transformed by the dynamic agency of the dream-work.

Dream-work is one of the watchwords of this book. Freud used the term as a heading under which he listed four distinct operations of transformation: displacement, condensation, symbolization, and secondary revision.[31] I will say more about each of these specific operations over the course of the chapters that follow, but for now it is important to emphasize the distinction between the dream-work and the dream-thoughts. The dream-work does not generate the dream's content, but rather works to *transfigure* it. Dream-work is a *treatment* of experience, in the artistic or chemical sense of the term—a kind of metamorphosis that, Freud realized, is one of our primary means to give meaning to experience. The dream-work can be thought of as a kind of archetype for the freedom of thought, in this respect, although this agency does not actually produce the dream-thoughts, but rather restricts itself to giving things a "new form." Freud regularly insisted that the essence of dreaming is this psychological work of transfiguration.[32] The 1925 footnote cited earlier emphasizes the point. After noting that dreams are nothing more than a "particular *form* of thinking," Freud adds, "It is the dream-work which creates that form, and it alone is the essence of dreaming—the explanation of its particular nature."[33] In short, Freud came to realize that the most radical aspect of dream-life was not *what* these experiences think, but *how* they think.

The significance of this distinction is readily evident in Mandela's nightmare. As the dreamer himself admits, the nightmare arose from a desperate wish to return home to see his family. This hardly seems surprising for someone facing lifetime imprisonment. Where the dream draws its poignancy and its potency is in *how* it negotiates this desire, *how* it dramatizes the experience of being severed from contact with human society. This severing was particularly extreme in the first few years of Mandela's prison sentence—when he was only allowed to receive one visitor and one letter every six months—but the process of his political isolation began long before his actual incarceration. In 1952, the future president was among a group of leaders who were banned by the Afrikaner government through its Suppression of Communism Act. Although this act specifically targeted Communists, it was worded broadly so as to include "any activity that allegedly promoted social, political, or economic change in South Africa." The banning aimed, in the short term, to prevent a variety of political figures from attending the national conferences of their respective parties. It was the first of a long series of bans that Mandela faced in the decade prior to his imprisonment.

Being banned in apartheid South Africa meant one's movements were severely restricted. Mandela was rarely allowed to leave his district of Johannesburg. It also prevented him from attending meetings of all kinds, not just political ones. He was prohibited, for instance, from attending his children's birthday parties or from speaking to more than one person at a time (both of which he defied the law to do). Banning was a kind of "walking imprisonment," and the strategy was one of the government's systematic attempts to immobilize leaders of groups who were resisting apartheid.[34] Whereas a government's banning a particular political organization is a common enough practice, the National Party's policy of banning *individuals* was unique among modern nations. Not since the Middle Ages had a government openly attempted to formalize this kind of juridical outlawry.[35] Apart from physical restrictions, banned persons were forced to resign any offices they held in any organization, and they were prohibited from speaking publically, or from writing for any publication. A banned person could not be quoted publicly and his photograph was prohibited from being circulated. Shortly before Mandela was due to be released in 1990, *Time* magazine produced an illustrated portrait of the leader on its cover because no new photographs of the freedom fighter had been available since the early 1960s. No one knew what the man looked like after decades of imprisonment. Or as *Time's* editor Robert L. Miller pointedly asked, "How do you capture the face of a man who has not been seen in public for the past 27 years?" His answer was to ask the artist Paul Davis to reimagine a portrait based on an earlier commission. (Four years prior, Davis had been asked to paint a portrait of the leader as a young man based on early photographs.) The magazine faxed a copy of the new portrait to Winnie Mandela for suggestions. The painter casually remarked that the process "was like the way police artists work."[36]

This challenge to the regime of representation tests the outer edges of what Jenny Edkins calls "face politics."[37] Banned individuals were denied legal safeguards in the event of disappearance or death. In effect, banning represented an organized political attempt to expunge a person from all aspects of social and public life, a gesture that sought to render an individual into a kind of *Homo sacer*—an accursed figure who is deprived of the usual entitlements and protections of human society. Mandela himself described this political act as an impingement of spirit: "Banning not only confines one physically, it imprisons one's spirit. It induces a kind of psychological claustrophobia that makes one yearn not only for freedom of movement but spiritual escape."[38]

Theorists such as Giorgio Agamben, Jacques Derrida, and others have analyzed the structural force of this kind of sovereign violence to great effect, but Mandela's dream offers a rather different site through which to consider its lived experience.[39] My phrasing here is deliberate: "lived experience" is a translation of the German neologism *Erlebnis,* which has been the subject of a long-standing philosophical debate. The term was coined in an effort to distinguish a particular category of experience that is distinct from the common use of this term (*Erfahrung*). In contrast to the usual sense of experience, *Erlebnis* refers to a kind of intensified experience, one that is rooted in feeling rather than an objective or otherwise detached rendering of the event. Mandela's nightmare, in this respect, offers a direct account of the experience of being banned without recourse to an empirical or philosophical description of this condition: the dream directly expresses the emotional experience of having one's very personhood scraped away.

Cover of Time *magazine, February 5, 1990. Illustration by Paul Davis.*

All dreams are individual accounts of lived experience in this respect—graphic re-presentations that allow for a more intimate grappling with one's condition.

For the philosophers, lived experience is properly understood as a category of consciousness.[40] Dreams, however, are a decidedly unconscious form of thinking. The material that composes the landscape of dream-life is often derived from those aspects of experience that the dreamer has either repressed or not yet emotionally processed. Indeed, part of the dream's aim is to bring to consciousness this "unthought known," to metabolize the experience in a way that makes it available as a form of emotional understanding.[41] Put differently, dream-thinking works to transform objective occurrences into subjective phenomena. Mandela's nightmare allowed him to articulate and to work through the emotional impact of his juridical sentence, rendering its impact in his own terms. This is one of our most intimate venues in which to exercise the freedom of expression.

The agency that performs this transformative labor is the dream-work. More specifically, Mandela's nightmare relied on *symbolization* to articulate the emotional significance of his experience of being erased from society. Symbolization (or what Freud initially named "considerations of representability") renders experience figuratively—presenting an idea or an emotion in pictorial terms. In the nightmare, Johannesburg was devoid of all people, all cars, and Mandela's home was turned into a ghost house. This empty landscape serves as a dramatic figure of the emotional experience of being banished. Mandela's experience of being barred from society, and of spending a great portion of his life imprisoned, felt akin to a world emptied of all human presence. In this respect, the nightmare gave form to the violence that imprisonment enacts, and more specifically, the violence that apartheid enacts: it figuratively conveyed the pain of depriving a human being access to the human world. For those it targets, apartheid transforms the world into a ghost town.

In more dramatic terms, the dream-work's elaborations serve as a protective shield against attacks on our being—whether biological or psychological traumas or social and political forms of aggression. As Arendt helps us to understand, political violence does not simply target the body of its subjects; it aims to destroy the subject's capacity to think. Political violence attacks the mental life of the citizenry. The dream-work's transfigurations attempt to work through these forms of aggression. The symbolic transformations aim to preserve our mental agency, in part by generating what

Didier Anzieu describes as a "psychic envelope," a secondary, protective skin for thought.[42] Mandela's recurring dream opened an interior landscape in which he had space *to think* about the terms of his political condition rather than be directly *equated* with it. The operations of dream-work helped shield and sustain his sense of self by enabling him to turn his political condition into a figure of thought. Or to use Mandela's own terms, this alternative mode of thinking helped him defend himself against that dimension of political violence that aimed to imprison his spirit. Dream-life, in this respect, can be understood as a primal form of resistance, indeed, as our most intimate model of civil defense. Freud famously described dreams as the guardians of sleep, but they are much more than that—these night watchmen preserve our psychic functioning, guard over our capacity to think, and in so doing, shield us against the world's impingements.

A caveat: dreams do not automatically issue in psychological growth. As several clinicians have shown, the dream-work function can be damaged, and when it is, our capacity to digest and process emotional experience is disabled. Indeed, many psychological events occur in sleep that greatly resemble dreaming but involve no unconscious psychological work: these events possess nothing of the *labor* of dream-thinking. Hanna Segal, for instance, describes patients whose dreams simply serve to evacuate unwanted emotions or ideas.[43] Analysts often distinguish, in this respect, between different degrees of symbol formation. The capacity to form and use symbols depends on the degree and nature of the communication that one has with one's internal objects. To cast this in Arendt's terms, one's capacity to think depends on one's capacity to establish a dialogue with oneself. It is a testament to Mandela's great strength of mind that he was able to use the solitude prison imposed to engage, as he put it, in "conversations with myself."[44]

A Discourse That Acts

Although easily overlooked, the disclosure of any dream relies on a fundamental act of translation: the conversion of the dream that is *dreamed in images* into the dream that is *articulated in words*. Dreaming is first and foremost an experience that takes place on an unconscious plane, usually under the cover of sleep. Narrating a dream is a secondary act of translation that occurs at some later point—presuming one has managed to smuggle the dream through that delicate border between sleep and awakening.

Freud was attentive to the way dream-thoughts are transformed into verbal expressions. His interpretations tend to focus on the ambiguity of language. In *The Interpretation of Dreams,* he frequently traces the various connotative nodes that issue from a single word in the dream-text.[45] However, it was one of Freud's contemporaries, Sándor Ferenczi, who first drew attention to the larger distinction between the experience of dreaming and the gesture of disclosing this experience to another person. Ferenczi was a Hungarian analyst in Freud's inner circle, and he became particularly attuned to the way people relayed their dreams. In 1912 he wrote that dreamers often feel impelled to convey their dreams "to the very person to whom the content relates."[46] This observation opened the door to a new understanding of dream-life as a special kind of communication *between* subjects. Whereas the activity of dreaming is a dialogue that one has with oneself, in the disclosure of this experience, a dream becomes a form of communication with another person—an unconscious avowal that involves both a sender and an addressee. In this way, reporting a dream is simultaneously a kind of publication of the dream-work and an action that moves the dream into another venue. Here dreaming becomes a speech act.

In clinical terms, dreaming represents an *intra*-psychic form of dialogue that takes place within the realm of the "dream-space," whereas the narration of a dream represents an *inter*-subjective form of communication that occurs between the dreamer and her interlocutor.[47] Contemporary clinicians are particularly attuned to the way patients communicate their dreams to the analyst. They take note, for instance, of the difference between a patient who reluctantly reports "I had a dream last night but only scraps of it are left" and a patient who eagerly expounds upon every detail of the previous night's adventures. The style in which one communicates a dream indicates a variety of things, including the relationship the dreamer has with her own dream-thinking, which is conveyed in the particular way she gives this object over to a third party for examination—or conversely, the way she withholds it.[48]

Not surprisingly, debate has ensued about the significance of this distinction between the act of dreaming and reporting the experience to another person. Is dreaming an experience that is designed to protect the privacy of the self? What, exactly, is being disclosed when one conveys a dream? How can reporting one's dream expose or perhaps even betray the self? Freud grappled with some of these questions early on. In the preface to the first edition of *The Interpretation of Dreams,* he explicitly asked his readers to grant him "the right of freedom of thought—in my dream-life, if nowhere else."[49] The entreaty refers to the fact that Freud had used his own dreams (as well as those of his patients) as the key source material for the book. This put him in something of a tight spot. As he acknowledges, "It inevitably followed that I should have to reveal to the public gaze more of the intimacies of my mental life than I liked, or than is normally necessary for any writer who is a man of science and not a poet." Here Freud is defending his unusual method and his unorthodox data. The preface closes with the plea to his readers to accept this situation and that if anyone finds any sort of reference to him or herself in the book, "grant me the right of freedom of thought—in my dream-life, if nowhere else."

Freud's concerns about public exposure spawns further questions when the dream under scrutiny belongs to the world's most famous political prisoner: What does it mean for Mandela to reveal the intimacies of his mental life to the public gaze? What does dream-life have to do with his capacity for the freedom of thought? And what does the freedom of thought have to do with the freedom of speech? What does it mean to *speak* of freedom? Or, indeed, how does one come *to be* free to speak of it?

These fundamental questions about the relationship between dreaming and the freedom of thought have a particular vector in the psychoanalytic clinic. In a trilogy of papers published between 1962 and 1976, the British-based psychoanalyst Masud Khan sought to find ways to return the experience of dreaming to the dreamer.[50] Khan came to believe that the role of the analyst should primarily be to help establish and support the patient's dreaming capacity, that is, to help patients gain more freedom in their symbolic functioning. Drawing from his clinical practice, Khan argued that patients who were unable to establish and effectively use the dream-space tended to exploit external reality as a venue to act out their unconscious conflicts and fantasies. A dream that enables an "actualization *in* the dream-space," Khan proposed, curtails "acting out in social-space."[51] By the end of his career, Khan had begun to view the distinction between the dreaming experience and the disclosure of a dream as a decisive one. In his last paper on the subject, he went so far as to describe the communication of the dream as a negation of the experience of dreaming: "Dreaming itself," he declared, "is beyond interpretation."[52]

Khan's close colleague, the French analyst J.-B. Pontalis, echoed some of these concerns and strongly disagreed with others. Pontalis admitted,

"In a sense, psychoanalysis strangles the eloquence of dream life."[53] But he took issue with Khan's move to privilege the dream experience at the expense of communicating the dream. Pontalis felt that attempts to cloister dream-life in the private, inner domain of the self deprive this experience of its primary function: *to bring conflicts to the surface*. For Pontalis, the act of interpretation is undoubtedly a symbolic wound to the privacy of the dreaming experience, but a wound that works in tandem with the dream-work's own procedures of substitution and transformation. Psychoanalysis, Pontalis emphasized, is a talking cure—a form of treatment that rests on the principle that the ability to freely speak to another person is integral to the relief of psychic pain.

In more general terms, almost every parent knows that getting a child to relay a nightmare helps to lessen some of its hallucinatory force. Relief arrives precisely because the dream that is captured in words is different from the dream as experienced. Translating and transmitting the experience of a nightmare helps to absorb the shock of the event. As Pontalis puts it, "The power of speech answers the imaginary power of the dream and takes its place."[54]

Dream-life becomes most *politically* potent in its verbal disclosure. Mandela reported his recurring nightmare in the context of his autobiography and, in so doing, aimed to establish a particular kind of relationship with his readers. (He sent a different iteration of this dream to his wife, Winnie, in a 1976 letter—a gesture that intended to establish a rather different kind of relationship.)[55] Language is, of course, a system of communication, but it is also an agency—an act that has consequences. Many verbal statements are designed simply to convey information, but as J. L. Austin taught us, some utterances have more concrete effects: a royal decree, a judge's ruling, an assessor's appraisal.[56] In each of these cases, the speaker uses language as an agency, as a means to perform an action.

As a lawyer and a banned figure, Mandela was well attuned to the performative power of language—and the language of the law in particular. Indeed, this intimacy was significant to his political practice. Early on in the freedom fighter's career, Mandela helped organize a wide-scale resistance movement that took aim at the Afrikaner government's institution of apartheid laws, the Population Registration Act and the Group Areas Act chief among them. These laws stripped people of their rights under the guise of preserving them. The ANC's Defiance Campaign staged demonstrations in which volunteers strategically defied some of these new laws:

marching through restricted areas without permits, entering railway stations through the "European's Only" entrance, and sitting on benches marked "Vir Blankes" ("For Whites"). The Defiance Campaign necessarily defined human beings as subjects of law, that is, as citizens who were being subjected to unfair apartheid policies. Because these laws positioned subjects in unequal ways in relation to the state, a vital part of the liberation struggle involved actively resisting these forms of subjugation.

The political principle behind the Defiance Campaign involves denying the sovereign authority of apartheid laws and creating instead, as one ANC statement phrased it, "conditions which will restore human dignity, equality and freedom to every South African."[57] The principle of defying an unjust law lies at the heart of civil disobedience: to oppose the law in order to transform it. But from where does the restoration of dignity arrive? From what sovereignty will the disenfranchised claim their franchise, if not from the law? The ANC's implicit answer (borrowed from Gandhi's example) is that the indivisible freedom of every South African is held *as a thought* in the gesture of defiance itself, even if the resources of liberation are not yet available. One might say that such gestures receive their authority from a freedom that is not present but whose existence is nevertheless indexed by the gesture. As the philosopher Jean-Luc Nancy suggests, "The thinking of freedom can only be seized, surprised, and taken from elsewhere by the very thing it thinks."[58]

Mandela's nightmare also demonstrates this characteristic "thinking of freedom." The disclosure exhibits the mechanics of the performative act that lies at the heart of this political wager—the elsewhere from which freedom springs. By its nature, dreaming carries us beyond the borders of the sovereign ego. Indeed, a nightmare is one of the more intimate experiences of being subjected to a foreign agency. This is precisely what makes these events so unsettling: the frightening images and sensations that arrive under the cover of sleep are not within the dreamer's command but rather arrive unbidden.

Disclosing this experience has a dual performative effect. First, the imaginary operations of the dream-work free up the linguistic structures that traditionally govern our capacity as speaking beings—dreams enable and provoke us to say things that we might feel otherwise unable to say. In this respect, the dream-work's re-formative power liberates the inhibitions and constraints of rational thought and speech—constraints that are particularly profound in dark times. The activity of dreaming is an exercise of the freedom of thought, and the disclosure of a dream *enacts* the freedom of speech.

Second, reporting a dream is an avowal of the dreaming experience. By disclosing his nightmare, Mandela testified to his lived experience; he affirmed *who* he was by placing himself in a particular relationship to his readers. Speaking with a view to freedom anchors the speaker within the web of human relations. The gesture establishes the structure of the relationship between subjects and sets the terms of political exchange. The intimate nature of Mandela's disclosure is signal in this respect. In 1994, the same year he was elected president, he made a list in one of his notebooks; the first item: "Personalize political experience."[59]

Our common world is borne on the backs of political actors who demonstrate the courage to disclose themselves to one another. By sharing his dream-life, Mandela reaffirmed this fundamental fact: the public sphere is created and sustained through such exercises of freedom.

Dreaming as a Practice of Freedom

Although promoted as an autobiography, *Long Walk to Freedom* was in large part the work of a collective. The original manuscript was begun clandestinely in 1974, while Mandela was still imprisoned on Robben Island. He describes writing deep into the night and in the morning, passing off finished sections to a handful of comrades who would add comments in the margins. Ahmed Kathrada, Mandela's longtime friend and fellow prisoner, describes "an editorial board" of trusted ANC members who worked collectively on the original draft, which was then transcribed into microscopic print and smuggled off the island in 1976. Then in the 1990s, after Mandela's release, the manuscript was adapted once again by an American journalist, Richard Stengel, with Kathrada and other advisers forming yet another collective to oversee the final editing process.[60] Although the narrative is written in first person, the Nelson Mandela we encounter in the autobiography is very much a *persona* in the ancient sense—a mask worn by a dramatic character in a play.

In this respect, *Long Walk to Freedom* belongs to the genre of what Philip Holden calls "national autobiography." These narratives work to ally the life of a leader with the process of decolonization. Other examples include Gandhi's *The Story of My Experiments with Truth* and Lee Kuan Yew's *The Singapore Story*.[61] This particular variation on the bildungsroman helps shape the new nation using the material of an imagined individual rather than an "imagined community," as Benedict Anderson famously proposed. The exemplary figure provides a model for the citizen to identify with and an example to follow. And for the newly democratic South Africa, this imagined individual was Nelson Mandela.

Given the collective authorship of the autobiography, the report of Mandela's recurring nightmare might best be thought of as an exemplar of "secondary revision"—that is, the editing of a dream so as to make a relatively coherent and comprehensive narrative. Secondary revision constitutes a second stage of the dream-work—a transformation that occurs during the dreamer's recounting of his or her dream. This revision could itself be understood as a form of censorship of the latent content, but as Freud points out in *Totem and Taboo,* this revision is also the result of trying to express unconscious modes of thinking using rational systems of thought.[62]

Long Walk to Freedom does not, in this respect, belong to the order of Marcus Aurelius's *Meditations* or Augustine's *Confessions.* This autobiography is not a book of personal thoughts, written to the author himself. It does not reveal the inner life of the icon, even as it trades on and stimulates the powerful desire to come to know something of Madiba's private struggles. (As any number of accounts show, Mandela was not introspective about his emotional life. He often became frustrated—and sometimes even angry—when prompted to discuss his feelings.)[63] While it might be tempting to cast Mandela's recurring nightmare as a rare glimpse into the great leader's otherwise impenetrable internal world, it is more in keeping with his own sensibility to treat this disclosure as simply another iteration of his political practice. Which is to say, recording and reporting his dream-life was just one more means to regulate and transform the constituent force of the political regime, a means to establish and preserve his own sense of sovereignty against apartheid's imposing force. Dream-life was one more venue Mandela used to exercise his indivisible sense of freedom.

Attending to one's dream-life as a form of political practice is not so much a new idea as a very old one. As Michel Foucault has shown, the ancient Greeks commonly exercised their civic liberty through a series of practical exercises—including dream interpretation. The exercises were sometimes formal practices such as pedagogical dialogue and the examination of one's conscience (which would later become confession under Christianity), but also included everyday gestures, such as style of dress, appearance, and gait. Near the end of his career, Foucault began a concerted investigation of these ancient "techniques of self" to grasp how the individual subject is able to constitute him- or herself in a way that is not reducible to external forms of domination. The project was ultimately left unfinished at the time of Foucault's death, but it nevertheless opened up a different dimension of political subjectivity, a new approach to thinking about the territory political life that drew from the inside of thought.[64]

One way that Foucault attempted to articulate this other dimension of political life was through a distinction he made between the process of liberation and what he called "practices of freedom":

> When a colonized people attempts to liberate itself from its
> colonizers, this is a process of liberation in the strict sense. But we
> know very well, and moreover in this specific case, that this process
> of liberation is not in itself sufficient to define the practices of
> freedom that will still be needed if this people, this society, and
> these individuals are to be able to define admissible and acceptable
> forms of existence or political society.[65]

This distinction directly echoes the position Mandela takes at the end of his autobiography, that closing note of hesitation in which the leader troubles the idea that freedom was achieved in South Africa with the advent of democracy. Neither thinker downplays the significance of liberation, but neither sees such victories as sufficient: liberation cannot define or even guide all the practical forms of freedom that will be needed for a viable life. As Mandela puts it, liberation is "the right not to be oppressed," but this is only the first step on a much harder and longer road: "to be free is not merely to cast off one's chains, but to live in a way that respects and enhances the freedom of others."[66]

In the ancient world, one of the most common ways to practice freedom in an everyday sense was through dream interpretation. Foucault's last work, *The Care of the Self,* opens with an extended discussion of the ancient methods of oneirocriticism. Gods gave advice, guidance, and, sometimes, explicit commands through dreams. For the ancients, these events constituted a form of guidance, and a high value was set on their decipherment. It was necessary to consult the countless professionals of nocturnal images, and it was also good to be able to interpret these signs for oneself, whether one was rich or poor, old or young, man or woman, private citizen or public official. Learning how to decipher these experiences was necessary to one's freedom, not because it somehow enabled one to get the better of destiny, but rather so one could weather the sufferings that would inevitably come. As one ancient writer put it, "When disasters come altogether and unexpectedly, they strike the spirit with so severe and sudden a blow that they overwhelm it; while if they are anticipated, the mind, by dwelling on them beforehand, is able little by little to turn the edge of sorrow."[67]

Dreaming provided a means for the dreamer to reflect upon such disasters and to contemplate his or her social existence. For the ancients, interpreting these nocturnal events was not a narcissistic exercise of introspection but an everyday means to carry out an examination of one's social moorings. Dreams display one's "style of activity," the position one tends to take with regard to others, indeed, one's larger way of being.[68] Reflecting on these thought-events provides a means to discover and reaffirm one's relation to oneself and to the world. Similar to the way external power relations are imposed through repeated coercive action, so the relation to oneself, which can bend these power relations, is established by practical exercises of freedom—everyday practices that a person might use to hone her relationship with herself.

Mandela's recurring nightmare was not a singular avowal in this respect. He regularly reported his dreams to his circle of comrades in prison; he shared them in letters to his intimates; he recorded them in his notebooks; he even jotted them down on the annual desk calendars that he used from 1976 to 1989:

8 DECEMBER 1976
Begin reading "Bury my heart" Dee Brown; sent letter U[niversity of] London

23 DECEMBER 1976
Zindzi's birthday

17 JANUARY 1977
Gossiping about others is certainly a vice, a virtue when about oneself.

20 JANUARY 1977
Dreamt of Kgatho falling into ditch and injuring leg

21 FEBRUARY 1977
Raid by approximately 15 warders under W/O Barnard[69]

These occasional entries represent another forum in which Mandela practiced his unique brand of civil disobedience, a quotidian technique he used
to reinsert himself into the human condition. Rather than treat his inner
landscape as somehow irrelevant to his political life, Mandela constantly
reinvented himself by turning the immediate condition of his unfreedom
back upon itself. By drawing from and nurturing that dimension of political subjectivity that is irreducible to the power relations imposed by the
state, he continually found ways to fold the force of apartheid, even as it
remained a force.

This is one more lesson that the great leader bequeathed to us: our
relation to others ultimately begins with the relation one has with oneself.
Attending to our dream-life is among our most intimate techniques of
tending this relationship, a technique of self-determination, a daily means
to practice self-governance, indeed, a paragon of freedom.

Dream Matters

The significance of dream-life has been slowly eroded throughout modernity. It is as if, in some strange way, this era's potent fantasies of rationalization, technological progress, and perfectibility have slowly claimed center
stage, displacing the older image of the human being as a small, frangible
creature that sleeps and dreams.

But dream we do. And Mandela's example reminds us of the significance
of attending to this alternative thought-landscape—especially in dark times.
There was little that was secret about the institution of apartheid in South
Africa. Yet, paradoxically, the malevolence at the heart of this political violence was by no means visible to all. This is because in such eras, such
violence is camouflaged by "the highly efficient talk and double-talk" of
official representatives, who, "in many ingenious variations, explain away
unpleasant facts and justified concerns."[70] Dark times are moments when
political violence occurs in full view of the public realm, when the sphere
of appearances is itself infected by a kind of black light. In these unyielding
climates, language is no longer used to disclose and expose but to obfuscate and hide what is. In dark times, under the pretext of upholding old
truths, a kind of official language emerges, a vehicle that is designed to

Page from Nelson Mandela's 1977 desk calendar. The entry for January 17 reads: "Gossiping about others is certainly a vice, a virtue when about oneself." The entry for January 20 is "Dreamt of Kgatho falling into ditch and injuring leg." Copyright Nelson Mandela Prison Collection, Nelson Mandela Foundation.

degrade truth, to sanction ignorance and preserve privilege, to stall conscience and thwart our capacity to think.

As Madiba taught us, dream-life becomes a particularly potent resource in such climates. The disclosure of his recurring nightmare quietly assures us that *dream-life matters*—it matters both for the individual and for our shared political lives. These uncanny mental events are vehicles for otherwise unthinkable thoughts and a wellspring for the freedom of speech. Dreaming is an indispensable species of psychological work that can help transfigure the force of a harsh reality. These thought-events are one of the principal means of transport for a unique form of knowledge that each subject carries but that remains vexingly other. And as Mandela's example shows, disclosing these events can become a political exercise that carries great force. In our own dark times, attending to this alternative form of thinking may just help us live through, resist, and ultimately transfigure our shared social and political landscapes otherwise.

CHAPTER 2

The Mother's Defense

The Dead Daughter in a Box Dream

SHE DOESN'T HAVE A PSEUDONYM like some of Freud's more famous patients. Her appearance in the historical record is brief enough that her anonymity has been preserved. I've taken to calling her Frau K (you'll see why in a moment). It's not known why she came to see Dr. Freud. The only record of her treatment we have is a fragment of a dream, although this fragment yields a surprising amount of information. Frau K was mother to a teenaged daughter and probably in her forties at the turn of the twentieth century. She almost certainly lived in Vienna, where Freud practiced. My impression is that the doctor was fond of her, but you can judge for yourself. Here is how she enters the annals of history:

When she was young she had been remarkable for her ready wit and cheerful disposition; and these characteristics were still to be seen, at all events in the ideas that occurred to her during treatment. In the course of the longish dream, this lady imagined that she saw her only, fifteen-year-old daughter lying dead "in a case." She had half a mind to use the scene as an objection to the wish-fulfillment theory, though she herself suspected that the detail of the "case" must point the way to another view of the dream. In the course of analysis she recalled that at a party the evening before there had been some talk about the English word "box" and the various ways it could be translated into German—such as *Schachtel* ["case"], *Loge* ["box at the theatre"], *Kasten* ["chest"], *Ohrfeige* ["box on the ear"], and so on. Other portions of the same dream enabled us to discover further that she has guessed that the English "box" was related to the German *Büchse* ["receptacle"] and she had been plagued by a recollection that *Büchse* is used as a vulgar term for the female genitals. If some allowance was made for the limits of her knowledge of topographical anatomy, it might be presumed, therefore, that the child lying in the case meant embryo in the womb. After being enlightened to this point, she no longer denied that the dream-picture corresponded to a wish of hers. Like so many young married women, she had been far from pleased when she became pregnant; and more than once she had allowed herself to wish that the child in her womb might die. Indeed after a fit of rage after a violent scene with her husband, she had beaten with her fists on her body so as to hit the child inside it. Thus the dead child was in fact the fulfilment of a wish, but of a wish that had been put aside fifteen years earlier. It is scarcely to be wondered at if a wish that was fulfilled after such a long delay was not recognized. Too much had changed in the interval.[1]

I admit, in my first few readings of *The Interpretation of Dreams* I passed over this passage without giving it much attention. I suspect this has something to do with Freud's tone. He seems oddly calm as he describes this young mother's wish for the death of her daughter, as if such thoughts were all too banal to really bother about.

In fact, it wasn't until I assigned the *Interpretation of Dreams* in one of my classes that the force of this dream registered. And then it was actually one of my students—an intelligent young man who could easily be described as remarkable for his ready wit and cheerful disposition—who made the force of Frau K's latent rage visible. One day, when the conversation had grown stagnant in the class, he drew our attention to this particular passage. He read the section aloud, and when this failed to arouse interest from his colleagues, he dramatically acted out the gesture of this young mother beating with her fists upon her own body, desperately wishing that the product of her unhappy marriage would die in utero—*in der Büchse.*

The student's empathy with this nineteenth-century Viennese woman was extraordinary to behold. I probably shouldn't speak for the class, but I think we were all stunned by his dramatic performance. Perhaps it was just the student's own latent rage and frustration that was on display that day, but then again, perhaps the emotional situation that engenders a dream is somehow inscribed in these fragile testimonies, affixed there by some mysterious resonance that ever awaits recognition. Either way, from that moment on, I felt I began to understand something new about the way violence begets violence, the way frustration born of grief can change the world in unpredictable ways.

Intergenerational Communication

Of course, Frau K didn't really try to kill her daughter. At best, her dream could be called an experimental kind of action: after all, a dream is just a dream. But it does seem strange that Freud says so little about the awful conflict that Frau K's vision harbored. He seems a little too preoccupied with putting this dream to use in defense of his theory that these visions represent the disguised fulfillment of an unconscious wish. *The Interpretation of Dreams* contains hundreds of dreams, and Frau K's dream might well have remained buried in the book. But Frau K's dream didn't stay buried. It reappears, again and again in Freud's work in a way that even the most famous dreams do not.

The first reappearance comes one hundred pages later in *The Interpretation of Dreams*. When Frau K's dream is recounted this time, Freud catalogs it under what he calls "typical dreams," and more specifically, under the class of dreams that "contain the death of some loved relative."[2] This method of cataloging dreams feels like something of an attempt to tame and contain these diaphanous objects. (His English editors extended the gesture after Freud's death, giving titles to all the dreams appearing in his collected works. This particular entry is indexed as the "dead daughter in case" dream.) When Frau K's dream returns in this latter instance, Freud reiterates his view that such dark thoughts belong to the past—and usually to a past that has been long abandoned. The unconscious, after all, knows no time. When the loved one appears in these dreams, the doctor muses, "they are not dead in our sense of the word but only like the shades in the Odyssey, which awoke to some sort of life as soon as they had tasted blood."[3]

In this instance, Freud offers a few more details about his patient's case history. He reports that behind Frau K's wish for the death of her daughter was an even earlier memory from the dreamer's childhood. When she was a small child, Frau K recalls hearing a story that her own mother had fallen into a deep depression during the pregnancy of which "she had been the fruit."[4] So there is a second layer of grief built into this dream: Frau K's mother also harbored a death wish for her unborn child. Freud's response to this uncanny repetition is equally brief: "When the dreamer herself was grown-up and pregnant, she merely followed her mother's example."[5]

"Merely" indeed.

Like sedimentary rock, Frau K's dream bears the extended deposits of a turbulent history that spans at least two generations. It manages to speak of the frustration and pain of a violent marriage and of a passionate wish to destroy the fruit of such a marriage. But the dream also carries a second, painful memory: the knowledge that the dreamer herself was unwanted, similarly subject to a mother's death wish. The dream registers this emotional information, or perhaps more accurately, it bears the memory of these wished-for deaths, giving form and shape to these shades from the underworld that come to life with the taste of blood. The dream displays the ways our most passionate conflicts can become split off from consciousness and transformed into fossils buried in the mind.

Indeed, this single dream manages to testify to any number of things, including the ways unacknowledged psychic pain can bind people to one another in captivity, going so far as to chain the fate of one generation to the next. And in this respect Frau K's oneiric vision works like a transport between worlds—between the land of the living and the land of the shades moored within her.

Symbolizing Infanticide

After making its debut in the pages of *The Interpretation of Dreams*, the "dead daughter in a box" dream quietly faded from public view. As far as I have been able to tell, this dream never received any further commentary as the book began to garner a larger audience in the decades after its publication. Frau K's dream is not among the handful of dreams that have become infamous, attracting continuous attention and analysis even decades later. By contrast, Freud's first "specimen" dream—the so-called dream of "Irma's injection"—has received thousands of citations and continues to be subject to passionate debate and reinterpretation more than one hundred years after its initial publication. This ceaseless speculation once prompted the French analyst J.-B. Pontalis to quip, "Poor Irma, will she never stop being given new injections of meaning?"[6]

Freud himself returned to Frau K's dream at least once more in his written work. The dream is recounted again after an interval of some fifteen years, this time in his *Introductory Lectures on Psycho-Analysis*. The title of this latter work refers to the fact that, by this point, Freud had secured a lecturer appointment at the University of Vienna, a position that carried the title *Professor Extraordinarius*. Herr Doktor Professor's class was a mixed group of doctors and laypeople of both sexes. In the winter of 1915–16, in the bitter midst of the First World War, Freud delivered what he decided would be his last course. The *Introductory Lectures* are essentially his lecture notes from this tumultuous year.

Freud spent several weeks lecturing on dream interpretation. One day the topic was "the archaic and infantile features of dreams." After reminding the class where he left off last time, Freud begins the lecture by speaking about "childhood amnesia"—the bewildering fact that we have almost no memory from the first years of life. One gets the sense that Freud is droning on to an indifferent audience and that he knows it, too, because he pauses to offer a pithy editorial comment: "There has not, in my opinion, been enough astonishment over this fact." Dreams, Freud goes on to say, have at their disposal this forgotten material from the first years of childhood. One imagines him taking a long pause before delivering this thunderbolt: "You will recall the amazement which was caused by our discovery that what instigates dreams are actively evil and extravagantly sexual wishes which have made the censorship and distortion of dreams necessary." If the audience had grown restless and bored, as lecture hall audiences are wont to do, one can imagine them suddenly becoming attentive. Finally Herr Doktor Professor is living up to his racy reputation. Freud continues by offering an example of an "actively evil" dream:

> A woman, whose dream meant she would like to see her daughter, now seventeen years old, dead before her eyes, found under our guidance that she had indeed at one time harboured this death-wish. The child was the fruit of an unhappy marriage which was soon dissolved. Once, while she still bore her daughter in her womb, in a fit of rage after a violent scene with her husband she had beaten with her fists on her body in order to kill the child inside. How many mothers, who love their children tenderly, perhaps overly-tenderly, to-day, conceived them unwillingly and wished at that time that the living thing within them might not develop further! They may even have expressed that wish in various, fortunately harmless, actions. Thus their death-wish against someone they love, which is later so mysterious, originates from the earliest days of their relationship to that person.[7]

Freud exhibits Frau K's dream to his class almost like a laboratory specimen, positioning the psychic object as evidence of that particular passionate bond we call "motherhood." The aggression and grief contained in the dream are generalized in a way that aims to show how maternal love can be freighted with a vertiginous intensity, indeed, which can even include "evil wishes" that aim to destroy the bond itself.[8]

It is no coincidence that a dream about infanticide would return to Freud's mind in the midst of the Great War. The doctor had two sons as well as any number of psychoanalytic followers in uniform. An entire generation of young men would be sent to their deaths. The British war poet Wilfred Owen would draw the link between war and infanticide more plainly in his "Parable of the Old Man and the Young." The short, chilling poem, written while Owen was on his way back to the Western Front after a traumatic breakdown, sets the Great War within a parable of the biblical story of the binding of Isaac—perhaps the paradigmatic case of infanticide. In Owen's version, as in the biblical account, an angel appears at the penultimate moment to stay the father's hand from sacrificing his son, commanding that a ram to be used in the boy's place. But in Owen's retelling, the old man ignores the angel's order, slays his son anyway, "and half the seed of Europe, one by one."[9]

Lecturing at virtually the same moment that Owen wrote these lines, Freud broaches the question of infanticide somewhat more guardedly. But like Owen's, the professor's point is that violence has a symbolic dimension. Indeed, Frau K's dream shares something of the sparse elegance of Owen's poem. Inside the pregnant mother is an actual fetus, of course, but there is also the internal *image* of a child, a psychic representation woven together from the mother's thoughts and desires, the unconscious memories of her own experience of early childhood, and from the violent situation of the gestation. In Frau K's case—but not only hers, of course—a war is occurring at the frontier between this inner dimension and the external reality of her condition. Violence is enacted in the material world, to be sure, but it draws upon the imaginary realm to gather its awful force. Here is where the potent work of dream-life comes in, generating, as it does, a bulwark between these sometimes hostile dimensions. Dreaming offers a potential place in which to be, *to exist,* in all the rich senses of that verb, which allows the dreamer to negotiate the conflicting demands of a hostile external reality and the relentless drives from the inside.

At its heart, *The Interpretation of Dreams* is a study of the formation and organization of dream-life, and more specifically, of the dream-work—the particular psychological operations that transform the dreamer's latent thoughts into the manifest content of the dream. These operations are readily evident in Frau K's case. Her dream borrowed directly from the day's residues; her inner ear became attuned to a particular fragment of the dinner conversation in order to give form to her conflicted thoughts and feelings about motherhood. More specifically, the dream made special use of one of the four forms of dream-work, what Freud originally termed "considerations of representability," or what is now more often simply described as symbolization. In Frau K's mind, the word "box" served as a substitute signifier for her womb. This idea was given symbolic representation—visually *figured*—through the transformation of the word into an image: Frau K dreams of her daughter, dead in a box. This word-image substitution allowed for the mental representation of an old conflict that still demanded expression.[10]

This is one of Freud's most significant discoveries: dreaming is a unique and vital thought-process, one of the fundamental means by which we are able to give *form to thought*. While the idea of aborting an unwanted pregnancy could not be openly acknowledged in fin de siècle Vienna, this otherwise inadmissible idea was given a stage in Frau K's dream-life. The significance of this gesture might be underscored by noting that abortion was not legalized in Austria until 1974 (and is still not covered by the government health care system today). The idea of spousal rape did not enter the legal system until the end of the twentieth century. In Frau K's time, marriage was understood to grant blanket sexual consent.

In short, this dream provided a home for an experimental thought that could not be thought otherwise. And on Freud's couch the dreamer found the courage to speak of it freely.

The Courage of Truth

It is something of an understatement to say that the mother is an overdetermined figure. The subject tends to draw exaggerated representations, either excessively idealized or excessively monstrous—or, indeed, both. As Alice Pitt notes, the mother "is represented as scorned and celebrated, excluded yet responsible, as bearing the promise of salvation but also as threatening engulfment."[11] Not surprisingly, the subject of motherhood has been one of the earliest and most sustained targets of feminist critique, in part, because not so long ago, becoming a mother was one of the few ways for a woman to enter civic life. Producing children established a woman's place in the household and enabled her to gain new economic and affective power.

As several of the Greek tragedies show, becoming a mother also afforded a woman the power to destroy the polis. In Medea's case, it was through the act of murdering her children by Jason (as well as her husband's new bride) that she managed to wipe out the future of the Corinthian ruling house. Infanticide, in this respect, can be understood as a political act—a means by which an ill-treated mother can rob her husband of the offspring who would perpetuate his name and lineage.[12]

In his 1983–84 lectures at the Collège de France, the French philosopher Michel Foucault explored another important civic role the mother performed in ancient Greece, namely, securing the citizen's right to speak in the polis. The 1983 lectures launched Foucault's inquiry into the notion of parrhēsia, which he defined as a particular form of speech that involves the courage of truth.[13] The element of courage was especially significant; Foucault never tired of emphasizing that *parrhēsia* is a unique form of address in that it necessarily involves some sort of risk for the speaker. When Antigone admits to defying the royal decree to bury her brother's body, for example, she exposes how Creon's tyranny is incompatible with justice, and in so doing, becomes a *parrhēsiastes*: a bearer of the truth. In this case, the price for Antigone's courage is her life. Less dramatically, Foucault speaks of those occasions when one takes the risk of telling a friend an unpleasant truth—something the speaker knows will put the friendship at risk. (He doesn't reference it, but the example brings to mind the bitter dispute Foucault had with his colleague Jacques Derrida over the question of madness.) For Foucault, *parrhēsia* is an irruptive, fracturing kind of speech that opens an undefined field of possibility between interlocutors and, as such, is indivisibly linked to courage and to freedom.

Part of Foucault's aim in these lectures is to show how this particular form of speech served as the forgotten basis of Athenian democracy. He notes that *parrhēsia* is not an exercise of power in itself but that it does have a central role in the polis as the grounds of the citizen's right to the freedom of speech. In this respect, the philosopher situates this activity of truth-telling as politically constitutive, both at the structural level of the city-state and in the dynamic relationship between citizens, what he began calling "the government of self and others."

During a lecture he delivered on the night of January 19, 1983, Foucault was engrossed in the question of where *parrhēsia* comes from. Exactly how does a citizen of Athens acquire this courage of truth, this right to speak freely? He turned to Euripides's ancient tragedy *Ion* for an answer. The play pivots on the title character's search for his identity. Ion was raised as an orphan by one of the priestesses of Delphi. As Foucault notes, this condition poses both a psychological and a political dilemma for the young man: on one hand, one cannot exercise the courage of truth without knowing oneself, without "self-knowledge" in the Socratic sense. On the other hand, the political right to speak freely in the city-state is transmitted through family lineage—only citizens have the right to employ *parrhēsia*. As Foucault points out, the play poses this dilemma concretely. Ion's laments, "If I do not find she who bore me, my life is impossible." *Parrhēsia*, the philosopher coolly observes, "must come from the mother."[14]

O, My Soul, Speak!

Enter Kreousa. Euripides describes this ancient queen of Athens as possessing a rare beauty and an unmatched grace, but like Frau K (you can see now where I've derived the sobriquet), her countenance is marred by a deep grief. Kreousa has, as one poet described, "the inhumanity of a meteor, sunk under the sea."[15] The nature of this inhumanity will be familiar given our intimacy with Frau K's "evil wishes." The chorus provides the queen's backstory at the outset of the play: as a young woman she was "seduced" by the god Apollo. Today we might call it rape. The difference was less defined for the ancients. For the ancients, using one's psychological, social, or intellectual abilities to seduce another person was judged to be no less criminal than using physical coercion.

At any rate, Apollo made sure Kreousa's father was kept in ignorance. And she, too, bore the secret, month by month, until it came time to give birth to the fruit of the seduction, whereupon Kreousa returned to the place where Apollo had initially brought her—a cave beneath the Acropolis in Athens. There, all alone, she gave birth to a son. And there, in a fit of maternal passion laced with shame, she abandoned the child, leaving it exposed to the elements to die. But unbeknownst to her, Apollo sent his messenger, Hermes, to save the child and to deliver him to Delphi, where he was raised as a servant of the temple without any knowledge of his identity. In the meantime, Kreousa married a foreign general named Xuothos in a match made to end a war. After many years, the couple found themselves unable to produce an heir and they voyage to Delphi to consult the oracle. The stage is set for a collision between a son looking for answers about his mother and a mother looking to reconcile her "ancient regrets" about her son.[16]

I won't rehearse all the intricacies of the play here, but suffice it to say the action turns on a case of mistaken identity. Misinterpreting the oracle's enigmatic message, Xuothos mistakenly believes Ion to be his son, a long-lost child of some drunken affair from his youth. When Kreousa hears of this, she is struck with rage and grief for this means her noble line will end and that the throne of Athens will pass to this bastard son. This leads to one of the most remarkable scenes of the play, which takes place at the gates of Apollo's temple. In a long moving speech, born from shame and humiliation and frustration, Kreousa bursts out with the truth. For Foucault, the scene is an exemplar of *parrhēsia*. And indeed, the struggle to find the courage of truth is dramatically evident. The confession is at once anxious and anguished. I challenge the reader to find a more vivid portrait of a soul in crisis:

> KREOUSA: Soul, soul, speak; nay, soul, O, my soul, be silent;
> how can you name an act of shame, an illicit act?
> soul, soul, be silent; nay, nay, O, my soul, speak;
> what can stop you, what can prevent?
> is not your husband traitorous?
> has he not stolen your hope and your house;
> all hope of a child is lost;
> great Zeus, O, great Zeus, be my witness;
> O, goddess who haunts my rocks,
> by Tritonis your holy lake, be witness;
> O, witness and help, O, stars, O, star-throne of Zeus;
> I have hidden too long this truth,
> I must lighten my heart of this secret;
> I must be rid of it.
>
> O, eyes, eyes weep, O, heart, heart break,
> you fell in a trap of men, you were snared in a god's net;
> (are gods or men more base?)

O, eyes, eyes weep, O, heart,
O, my heart cry out against him of the seven-strung lyre,
against him of the singing voice;
yes to you, you, you I shout
harmony rhythm, delight of the Muses,
you I accuse; you, born of Leto,
you bright traitor within the light;
why did you seek me out, brilliant, with gold hair?
vibrant, you seized my wrists, while the flowers fell from my lap,
the gold and the pale-gold crocus,
while you fulfilled your wish,
what did it help, my shout of mother, mother?
no help came to me in the rocks;
O, mother, O, gold flowers lost;

O, terror, O, hopeless loss, O, evil union,
O, fate, where is he whom you begot?
(for fear of my mother, I left the child on those bride-rocks;)
O, eyes, eyes, weep,
but that god will not relent, who thought of the harp-note
while his child was done to death by hovering eagles or
        hawks;
O, heart, heart beak,
but your heart will never break,
who sit apart and speak prophecies;
I will speak to you on your golden throne,
you devil at earth-heart, your golden tripod is cursed;

O, evil lover, you grant my husband who owes you naught,
his child to inherit my house, while my child and your child is lost;
    our son was torn by beaks of ravaging birds,
he was caught out of the little robes I wrapped him in, and lost;

O terror, O hopelessness, O evil union, O fate,
I left him there on the rocks, alone in a lonely place,
be witness, O, Delos, and hate, hate him you palm-branch,
caught with the leaves of the laurel to bless that other so-holy birth,
    yours, Leto's child with Zeus;

Heart, heart weep, soul, O my soul, cry out,
harmony, rhythm, delight of the Muses,
you, I accuse who pluck from the soulless frame of the harp,
the soul of the harp.[17]

Upon hearing this awful confession, Kreousa's companion, her father's old tutor, is overcome with emotion. One suspects the tutor functions as a stand-in for Kreousa's own father, who surely would not have been able to bear this testimony. What father could bear to hear that his daughter was raped and bore a child all alone so many years ago? A remarkable dialogue ensues in which more details emerge. Over the course of the conversation, Kreousa's guilt is set to one side. By the conclusion of the scene, the old man, so full of rage, insists on taking revenge against the god. Kreousa is hesitant but eventually relents and a plot is hatched to poison Ion at the evening's banquet. Here is where the element of tragedy comes in.

As Foucault points out, the *parrhēsia* operates on several levels in this scene. Most obviously is Kreousa's tirade against Apollo, which represents a specifically juridical form of *parrhēsia*: a public accusation concerning an injustice. There is an important element of asymmetry here insofar as the accused is much more powerful than the accuser. This is a familiar political dilemma: what can the oppressed do in the face of a much more powerful oppressor, when she has no means of retaliation, when she is too weak to fight to redress the wrong? She can speak. At risk and grave danger to herself, she can stand up before the person who committed the injustice and *speak*. And indeed, Kreousa does dare to speak freely of her oppression: she publicly accuses the god at the very doorstep of his own temple. In this way, *parrhēsia* is, Foucault suggests, a "human practice, a human right, and a human risk."[18]

It bears emphasizing that this form of juridical *parrhēsia* does not just belong to the ancient past. It still operates in the contemporary age, for instance, in the testimony given at the United Nations' International Criminal Tribunal for the former Yugoslavia. One of the tribunal's trials sought to prosecute four Serbian soldiers for rape as a crime against humanity. This was the first time in history that an international court tried such a charge. The prosecution turned, in large part, on the testimony of a handful of women from the town of Foča, who summoned the courage to speak of their systematic sexual enslavement. The transcripts of these testimonies, like Kreousa's speech, carry all the harrowing effects of an injury that

cannot be presented directly, but whose force is nevertheless felt in its be-
lated effects, in all the fragile irruptions and breakdowns of speech, which
simultaneously command and defy our witness. When Kreousa speaks of
the "gold flowers lost," we understand her meaning. At The Hague at the
turn of the twenty-first century, the women had to be more direct. When
the prosecuting lawyer asked Witness 87 (whose identity was protected
by the mandate of the court) what happened after she was raped by the
Serb soldiers who captured her, she answered, "They asked me if I was a
virgin." When she answered that she was "until a few moments ago," she
was ordered to her to take her clothes off again, whereupon four more soldiers raped her.[19]

There is, of course, much more to be said about the function of avowal
in the process of justice. For now let us just note that this remarkable form
of speech, this courage of truth, still serves as a central pivot in the matrix
of political discourse, even today, at the dawn of the third millennium.

Practices of Freedom

Perhaps you have guessed, by now, my interest in pairing these scenes,
these women: Freud's patient, Frau K, and Foucault's muse, Kreousa. Both
of these women faced a similar conflict and both became word bearers of
a difficult truth. But while these women bear an extraordinary affinity,
it must be acknowledged that the men with whom they traveled do not.
Foucault's antipathy for the "disciplining" techniques of psychology would
have been well known to his audience, and he was, at best, circumspect
about psychoanalysis (even as he shares a few, faint words of praise for
the French analyst Jacques Lacan in these late lectures). But even if these
two thinkers were not particularly compatible, the body of their thought,
or perhaps I should say the maternal bodies animating their thought—the
sheer vitality and transforming force of these two women, the Viennese
dreamer and the ancient queen of Athens—allow us to bring them into
conversation.

At the end of his life, Foucault staked his thought on the wager that
parrhēsia serves as the grounds of a democracy worthy of the name. Although the citizen's right to the freedom of speech would seem to be con-
stitutionally given, the philosopher showed, via Euripides, that this right
must be actively *forged,* that this is a form of speech born of passion, painfully extracted, often at the expense of excruciating shame or grave danger.

In this respect, Foucault makes a strong distinction between the problems of law, which script constitutional rights and freedoms for abstract citizens, and the problems of politics, which lean on the character of specific human players. What interested Foucault was the latter, and especially *parrhēsia*, that specific speech act that indexes the subject to the truth, and which powerfully structures the speaker's relationship to herself and others. It is this theatrical arena of politics that Foucault began to distinguish as "the government of self and others."

Frau K's grappling with her dream-life also places her within this political theater. But where this woman's story differs from the dramatic staging of Euripides's play is the vehicle by which this *parrhēsiastes* arrives at the courage of truth. Unlike Kreousa, the truth comes to Frau K in an alienated form—through a dream. We should be wary of rarifying this object. Frau K's dream of her daughter dead in a box could mean any number of things; indeed, this was precisely Freud's point when he insisted that all dreams are "overdetermined," that they have any number of sources and significations. Any attempt to pin down some ultimate meaning is not only impossible but also contrary to the point. Rather the significance of a dream emerges in the transposition of the event into words, in the chain of associative memories and thoughts that comes to mind. In Frau K's case, grappling with this dream led her to disclose a painful experience to Dr. Freud: when she became pregnant in the midst of a violent, unhappy marriage, she wished her unborn child would die in her womb.

The stakes of this disclosure are not simply the remembrance of things past. As Foucault helps to show, what is more important here is the enactment of a particular form of speech in the present, for here is where meaning is fashioned, or more accurately, *refashioned*. Frau K effectively reconstituted her reality through her grappling with her dream. Or rather, she was *intersubjectively reconstituted within it*, for this speech involves an address to the other and a negotiation with "It"—the structuring force of the unconscious. In this, Frau K's efforts bear a striking similarity to the freedom of speech that Foucault describes: each woman struggled to articulate a powerful emotional truth, an experience whose verbal conveyance profoundly restructured the speaker's relationship to herself and others. As Jacques Lacan compactly phrased it, "One changes the course of [her] history by modifying the moorings of [her] being."[20]

There are, in fact, two distinct moments here, two kinds of negotiation required to modify the moorings of one's being. The first involves the *intra*-subjective activity of dreaming, the process of symbolization that is the dream-work. The second involves the *disclosure* of this experience, the speaker's particular *use* of her dream as a mode of *inter*-subjective communication.

Before coming to see Dr. Freud, Frau K did not know what ailed her. Presumably this is why she called upon the doctor. But contrary to most modern forms of medical treatment, the psychoanalyst does not dispense a prescription to the patient. The cure does not arrive from elsewhere. Rather it is the patient herself who provides the material for the treatment. The analyst's role is to listen and to facilitate this talking cure. The facilitation is not neutral, of course; the analyst is an object of transference, which is no small matter. But as many psychoanalytic theorists have suggested, this treatment is perhaps best understood as a site for the support and strengthening of the patient's dreaming function, which is to say, the subject's capacity to symbolize his or her own conflicts.[21] One of Freud's foundational discoveries was the recognition that dreams are one of the primary means by which human beings undertake this activity.

Dreaming is also, of course, a close encounter with the unconscious. In reporting the dream, "It" manifests in our discourse; indeed, "It" speaks through us. The recognition of the presence of this force in human life has considerable consequences in social and political terms. Rather than casting one's misfortunes as a matter of fate or a vengeful action of the gods, taking the unconscious into account means accepting that the human condition entails being subject to this other agency that cannot be possessed, which cannot even be grasped directly, and yet nevertheless exerts powerful effects.

The second, *inter*-subjective moment—the dreamer's use of this diaphanous object as a means to communicate with others, the symbolic disclosure of the dream—renders this process into a political matter proper. As Hannah Arendt emphasized, "With word and deed we insert ourselves into the human world, and this insertion is like a *second birth*."[22] Like Foucault, Arendt emphasized that true speech works to reveal *who* the speaker is. Politics, for both theorists, turns on the disclosure of the agent of speech. Arendt tirelessly insisted that political theory overlooks this relatively simple fact: human beings must willingly disclose themselves as the subjects of their speech, as distinct and unique persons, and that our political life together depends on this web of human relationships. For Arendt, moreover, the actualization of the human condition corresponds to the fact of birth. It is precisely because we are born—and that with each birth something uniquely new comes into the world—that we are able to conceive of something like freedom. Arendt simultaneously purged and grounded this concept, treating freedom not as a transcendental idea or as an intrinsic property of subjectivity. Rather freedom is something conditioned by human existence itself, a result of having been born: "The very capacity for beginning is rooted in *natality*, and by no means in creativity, not in a gift but in the fact that human beings, new men, again and again appear in the world by virtue of birth."[23]

When Frau K claimed her right to the freedom of thought by disclosing her dream, she effectively reinserted herself into the web of human affairs, transposing her private concerns into the material of the social fabric. The gesture is more than a little akin to the "second birth" that Arendt situates as the grounds of the political realm. Dreams weave a womb around what ails us, providing a container for painful or traumatic experiences. Through the symbolizing activity of the dream-work, dreams give this indigestible material a new form. This transformation, like birth, implies perennial beginnings.[24] And then, in the secondary act of transposing this mental-event into words, the speaker discloses and exposes her commitments to her social situation and establishes a particular relationship to her interlocutors. The commitment involved in such speech acts entails a risk, indeed, the courage of truth.

Unfortunately, the historical record does not afford us access to the rest of Frau K's story. We will have to be content with wondering how her struggle affected the rest of her life. I would be willing to wager that, like Kreousa, Frau K's claiming of her role as *parrhēsiastes* had a profound effect on the next generation—that her daughter's future, like that of young Ion, was set free by her mother's courage to speak the truth.

Perhaps it is a form of historical idealism to return to the problem of truth-telling in the political sphere. As Arendt once dryly noted, "No one has ever doubted that truth and politics are on rather bad terms with each other."[25] But then again, perhaps in our contemporary moment, which is so disillusioned with freedom and truth, dream-life might just offer a new horizon to play this old game of politics, a place from which these ancient questions might be revisited anew.

CHAPTER 3

The Soldier's Defense

The Gassed Man Dream

Only a military hospital can really show you what war is.

—Erich Maria Remarque, *All Quiet on the Western Front*

AT THE BEGINNING OF APRIL 1917, Second Lieutenant Wilfred Owen was headed back to the Western Front alongside his Manchesters battalion. The subaltern was barely twenty-four years old. He had not yet composed "Dulce et Decorum Est" or any of his war poems. But as the popular account goes, 1917 marked the beginning of Owen's *annus mirabilis,* the year in which he would find his voice and become *the* poet of the Great War. As Cecil Day Lewis once vividly described, "The subject made the poet: the poet made poems which radically changed our attitude towards war."[1]

Such dramatic descriptions are not uncommon, but they mark a certain distance from the war. It is a retrospective fantasy to claim that Owen's searing experiences at the front instilled a special capacity to express "the truth untold / The pity of war, the pity war distilled"—or indeed, that his poems would generate a sea change in the sensibilities of a generation yet to come.[2]

Owen's work offers plenty of evidence of what his beloved fellow poet John Keats once described as "Negative Capability"—that is, the ability to tolerate discomfort and uncertainty without demanding its resolution.[3] But it is perhaps more accurate to say the subject *maimed* the poet; Owen's so-called *annus mirabilis* could just as easily be described as his *annus horribilis.* The young man spent the greater half of 1917 in a suburb of Edinburgh at Craiglockhart War Hospital for Neurasthenic Officers. Neurasthenia was the official new term for a condition popularly known as shell shock—what we now call post-traumatic stress disorder (PTSD). The neurasthenia label was introduced into the British military after the Battle of the Somme. Among other things, this siege provoked enormous numbers of

Portrait of Wilfred Owen by unknown photographer. Copyright the English Faculty Library, University of Oxford and The Wilfred Owen Literary Estate.

cases of psychological breakdown—some thirty thousand men, by some accounts—which forced the authorities to revise their early opinion that this condition only affected "degenerates."

In truth, praise of Owen's work only arrived belatedly. At the time, his own commanding officer called his nerve into question. And when his poems were first published after the war—posthumously because Owen was killed in action just a week before the armistice—his first readers dismissed them as the work of a "broken man." His chief biographer, Dominic Hibberd, describes how his early supporters scrambled to deflect attention away from the hospitalization when readers initially rejected his work as "the self-pitying complaints of a coward."[4]

The difference between these two narratives seems dramatic: how does someone initially considered a coward become *the* voice of a generation? It is tempting to explain away the early judgments of the poet's character as simply belonging to the prejudices of the era. A century later, it might seem easier to distinguish between cowardice and shell shock. We have learned a great deal more about psychological trauma over the course of the twentieth century. During the Great War, the difference was less clear. In the trenches and on the battlefield, Owen did not lack for bravery; the historical record is clear on this point. But away from the front he suffered a breakdown that left him stammering, shaking, and haunted by night terrors. Can one be afflicted with these soul-rending fears and still be said to be courageous? Or to come at this question the other way around: what if Owen's ability to tarry with his fear was precisely what lent the poet's voice its force?

As Hannah Arendt once wrote, "Courage is a big word," and there is more to it than "the daring of adventure which gladly risks life for the sake of being as thoroughly and intensely alive."[5] In *The Human Condition*, Arendt describes courage as indispensable to political action. Such a claim is not unique. Countless thinkers, from Aristotle to Winston Churchill, have espoused as much. But unlike these other thinkers, Arendt does not champion the familiar definition of this virtue. She was not interested in courage as a species of physical fearlessness or unimpeachable moral integrity. Instead, she singled out something she named "original courage"— this is a kind of bravery that is "not necessarily or even primary related to a willingness to suffer the consequences," but instead turns on a readiness to show "*who one is, in disclosing and exposing oneself*."[6] For Arendt, this primary willingness to unveil oneself—to bare one's soul before others—

serves as the firmament of our political life together. What is more, she writes, "The extent of this original courage, without which action and speech and therefore, according to the Greeks, freedom, would not be possible at all, is not less and may even be greater if the 'hero' happens to be a coward."[7] Original courage is not the absence of cowardice. Rather, in Arendt's mind, this indispensable virtue is something that is woven out of the very fabric of one's fear.

My intent in this chapter is to treat Owen's struggle with his symptoms—his willingness to publicly disclose and expose his terrors of the soul—as an exemplar of the "original courage" that Arendt championed as the grounds of the polis. By drawing attention to the poet's fear I realize I might seem to be siding with his earliest critics. Regardless, I think the significance of his work lies less in his realistic descriptions of the trenches than in his portrayal of the ravaged landscape of the mind, in his willingness to linger over the terror that crippled so many soldiers. Owen did not pen any grand antiwar declarations like his idol Siegfried Sassoon. But he nevertheless did embody the courage of truth in his willingness to disclose and expose his inner torments. Owen dared to make his most private means of defense public. More specifically, he revealed the intimacies of his dream-life to the public gaze, transforming these inner experiences into catholic communications, and in so doing, gave voice to an integral aspect of the human condition.

An exemplar is both an ideal and a figure that is meant to stand in for the many. My privileging of Owen is not designed to champion him as a singularly authentic voice. Indeed, as much of the scholarship on his work shows, his poetry is best understood intertextually, that is, as a profound crossing of texts and voices, a polyphony that was multiplied by his contact with the staff at Craiglockhart and his encounter with the more established poet, Sassoon. The larger question at stake here—indeed, in the book as a whole—involves how internal events such as dreams can yield evidence for the ways individuals forge a relationship with the social fabric—or, indeed, how we are *forged by* our milieu. The broad-scale transformation of soldiers' dream-life during the Great War testifies to the profound psychological effects of this conflict. The sheer force of this war *impressed* itself at the most intimate levels of human existence. Owen's dreams are not particularly unique in this catalog, but he did make particularly good use of them. His extraordinary rendering of his dream-life provides important clues about how social and political aggression registers at the level of the individual psyche. And more significantly, Owen's work shows us how dream-life can provide a singular means of defense. This thought-landscape can serve as a location to exercise one's agency when the horizon of freedom seems all but eclipsed.

This century-old exemplar remains timely. Accounts of soldiers in psychic crisis are back in the news headlines. Across the Allied countries, suicides among military personnel have risen exponentially in the past decade.[8] One hundred years after the Great War, we no longer speak in terms of "gallantry in the face of peril." "Extraordinary rendition" has a rather different meaning and no one is shot for cowardice anymore—at least not officially, although one is tempted to say that today's soldiers simply enact this sentence upon themselves. Like the symptoms of shell shock, suicide contains a symbolic communication. In killing oneself, the subject attempts to send a message to the other: an acknowledgment of guilt, a desperate appeal to be heard, a means to enact revenge. The messages are multiple and overdetermined.[9] But today's military officials seem just as baffled about the meaning of these unconscious statements as they were during the Great War's epidemic of shell shock. And if anything, the horizon of freedom provided by dream-life is granted even less significance than in Wilfred Owen's day. One suspects "the truth untold" presses evermore urgently now, just as then.

The Casual

It was during the Allied offensive on Saint Quentin, in April 1917, that Wilfred Owen's nerves gave way. The winter of 1917 was said to be the worst winter France had known for forty years. At the beginning of April, Owen's battalion was rushed up to the front—to the *Siegfriedstellung* or "Hindenburg Line" that marked the new Western Front after the Battle of the Somme. As he reports in a letter home, Owen's company went "over the top" twice in one day. Never before had the battalion encountered such intense shelling: "The reward for all this," he wrote to his mother, "was to remain on the Line for 12 days":

> For twelve days I did not wash my face, nor take off my boots, nor sleep a deep sleep. For twelve days we lay in holes where at any moment a shell might put us out. I think the worst incident was one wet night when we lay up against a railway embankment. A big

shell lit on top of the bank, just 2 yards from my head. Before I
awoke, I was blown into the air right away from the bank! I passed
most of the following days in a railway Cutting, in a hole just big
enough to lie in, and covered with corrugated iron. My brother
officer of B Coy, 2/Lt Gaukroger lay opposite in a similar hole. But
he was covered with earth, and no relief will ever relieve him, nor
will his Rest be a 9 days-Rest.[10]

Owen slips in and out of present tense throughout this account, a tem-
poral disturbance that speaks to the ongoing, persistent intensity of the
incident—as if it were *still* happening. Second Lieutenant Gaukroger had
been killed a few days before and the body had been duly buried. In
another letter written to his sister, Owen cryptically describes how he
lived "so long by poor old Cock Robin (as we used to call 2/Lt. Gaukroger)
who lay not only near by, but in various places around and about, if you
understand. I hope you don't!"[11] Owen is characteristically both obscure
and revealing here: the shelling that blew him into the air also disinterred
Gaukroger's body. Flight being impossible, it seems he was forced to spend
several days in awful proximity to the scattered remains of the corpse.[12]

By April 22, Owen's battalion finally left the front line, retreating eight
miles to Quivières for a "Rest" period. Owen was still dizzy from the incident at the embankment. By May 1, he was "observed to be shaky and
tremulous, and his conduct and manner was peculiar, and his memory con-
fused."[13] These are the only symptoms recorded in his personnel file. In a
letter to his mother, he admits being "sent down" by the doctor, but asks
her to tell no one that he is a "Casual"—that is, deemed medically unfit to
return to action.[14] Owen was reticent to disclose details about his state,
even to his mother, with whom he shared an otherwise involved corre-
spondence. (More than eighty percent of his surviving letters are addressed
to her.)[15] Owen's reticence is not surprising given the climate of the time;
shell shock was considered to be a disgrace. In his 1929 autobiography,
Good-Bye to All That, Robert Graves reported that Owen was accused of
cowardice by his commanding officer, a judgment that a left lasting scar on
the young man.[16] Although Owen was never in any real danger of being
court-martialed, this could be a serious, indeed, deadly charge: by the time
of the armistice, some three thousand British soldiers had been convicted
by courts-martial for cowardice, desertion, and other crimes, and of these,
some 346 were executed.[17] After the war, on both sides of the conflict, official

judicial commissions were organized to inquire into shell shock. The neb-
ulous distinction between this condition and cowardice was one of the
chief topics, precipitated by an enduring anxiety that there had been, as
one British commissioner put it, "injustices done in the early stages of
the war."[18]

It is somewhat jejune to say that the Great War challenged many of
the inherited social and cultural ideas of the time—including our understanding of the fragility of the human psyche. Wyndham Lewis once called
it "the turning-point in the history of the earth."[19] It doesn't take long
before such phrases start to ring hollow. But the expression is apt in that it
figures the war as a profound, shattering force that splintered the course of
human history. The profundity is not just in the scale of the destruction
but also in its character. In Owen's case, the incident at the railway embankment radically disorganized something in him, disturbing his very claim
to subjectivity. Perhaps because it was impossible to flee the horrid aftermath of the explosion—because he could not escape the wretched remains of old Cock Robin—that part of his own personality deserted him
instead. We cannot know precisely what happened to him during those
two days he spent under the haze of a concussion, when he was trapped in
a hole just big enough to lie in, with gruesome bits of his brother officer
lying around and about. What we do know is that afterward he became a
stranger to himself. Uncontrollable symptoms arouse out of this wounding. Something wholly other began to inhabit the young man, something
that seemed to be born from the event, indeed, *of* the event. And this otherness *showed itself* through tremors and stammering, and in nightmares and
hallucinations.

Etiology in Dispute

Owen's symptoms were not particularly unique. Not only did thousands
of other soldiers share them on the Western Front, there is an extended
catalog of battle dreams that can be found in the historical record. When
Shakespeare writes of Queen Mab spiriting over the soldier's neck, he
dreams of cutting foreign throats: "Of breaches, ambuscadoes, Spanish
blades, Of healths five-fathom deep," until he is abruptly awoken, "frighted"
by the sound of "drums in his ear."[20] Herodotus mentions terrifying battle dreams in his *Histories*. They also figure in Hippocrates's work and in
Lucretius's poetry.[21] During the Napoleonic Wars, French soldiers spoke

of being haunted by the eerie *vent du boulet,* or what the English called "cannon-fever"—the peculiar "whistling, dangerous, spinning sound" of cannonballs rushing past, a horrible feeling that entered through one's ears.[22]

There is vociferous debate about how to interpret this litany of symptoms. Military psychiatrists have diverging opinions about whether each war produces its own distinct set of disorders related to the technological and cultural changes. Some insist that there are no new symptoms, while others believe that each war brings new kinds of exposures, which in turn produce new kinds of "syndromes."[23] The Great War is significant to this debate because it is generally regarded as the birth of military psychiatry— and the issue that dominated this origin was shell shock.

The language of diagnosis varied—in England, doctors spoke of "neurasthenia"; in France and Germany, it was *névrose de guerre* and *Kriegsneurose,* respectively—but the larger clinical picture was compellingly uniform. In 1915, in the well-known British medical journal the *Lancet,* Charles Myers began reporting symptoms that were being observed on both sides of the conflict: loss of memory, vision, smell, and taste.[24] In 1917 the German psychiatrist Robert Gaupp similarly observed "states of sudden muteness, deafness . . . general tremor, inability to stand or walk, episodes of loss of consciousness, and convulsions."[25] Gaupp's patients' symptoms, like those of Myers's patients, seemed to have arisen in relation to shells exploding in their immediate vicinity. But the symptoms baffled the military doctors because they tended to appear some time *after* the initial incident, indeed, in Owen's case, while away from the immediate dangers of the trenches. Several cases were preserved on film by Arthur Hurst, a doctor who worked at Seale Hayne Military Hospital in Devon. The footage is a remarkable visual record of the physical manifestations of shell shock, but this outward, visible expression of the condition cannot explain its psychological cause.[26]

The sheer number of the "new wounded" overwhelmed both sides.[27] By 1916 the British army was suffering from an epidemic of Casuals, which created a manpower crisis. Desperate measures were introduced by the military authorities—including the conscription of civilian doctors. Even the small group of psychoanalysts that had gathered around Freud in Vienna were mobilized into the medical corps by 1916. Like the war itself, debate raged about how to treat these cases, and indeed about what, precisely, was wrong with the soldiers. Doctors hypothesized two different kinds of cause, positions that were reflected in the varying terminology.

Beginning in 1915, but widespread after the Somme, the use of the term "shell shock" implied a belief that the symptoms had an organic-mechanistic cause arising from pathoanatomical disturbances. In other words, the tremors, stammers, muteness, and blindness were presumed to be the result of microscopical destruction of the tissue and hemorrhages in the brain—the central organ of the nervous system. This thesis borrowed from earlier neurological discussions of "railway spine" (a similar condition that appeared in relation to railway accidents.)[28]

When doctors used the term "war neurosis" there was usually an implied psychological aspect to the shock (as with peacetime neurosis). In this case, the motor symptoms were believed to have an underlying *psychic* cause. As the German head-of-hospital at Posen, Ernst Simmel, put it in 1918, "The physical sensitivity is merely the external symptom of an internal, strongly repressed affect. . . . Whatever in a person's experience is too powerful or horrible for his conscious mind to grasp and work through, filters down to the unconscious level of his psyche. There it lies like a mine, waiting to explode the entire psychic structure."[29] Within these two camps, the question of whether the casualties were malingerers did not go away, which is to say, the question of cowardice was never far from the minds of the doctors—or their patients. Etiology aside, the various treatments for the condition seemed to be informed by each particular doctor's sense of the demands of war.

Dr. Lewis Yealland, for instance, a Canadian doctor who treated Allied soldiers at the National Hospital in London, published an account of his approach in the *Lancet* in 1917. The article, coauthored with another doctor, provides justification for their method: "adequate treatment is essential and it will make all the different between a useless burden to the State and a useful citizen or even a useful soldier."[30] Like many others, Yealland promoted a treatment that combined "suggestion" with "faradization" (an induced form of electric shock) as the most effective method of "re-education." Yealland surmised that the treatment turned on the patient's faith in the doctor's ability to cure. When this faith was in doubt, "The current can be made extremely painful if it is necessary to supply the disciplinary element which must be invoked if the patient is one of those who prefer not to recover."[31] Several illustrative cases—including an example of "functional mutism" in a twenty-four-year-old private—are recorded in detail in Yealland's book, *Hysterical Disorders of Warfare*, published in 1918. The private in question had been unable to speak for nine months, and as Yealland notes, many previous attempts had been made to cure him, including being "strapped down in a chair for twenty minutes at a time, when strong electricity was applied to his neck and throat; lighted ciga-rette ends had been applied to the tip of his tongue and 'hot plates' had been placed at the back of his mouth." All such attempts were unsuccessful. Then, in a scene that seems to be straight out of the Inquisition, Yealland recounts how he conquered this resistant war neurotic by applying "shock after shock to the posterior wall of the pharynx" and relentlessly com-manding the patient to speak. The doctor's account of the four-hour treat-ment spans some eight pages.[32] When Pat Barker borrowed this scene for her war novel *Regeneration,* the only change she made to Yealland's own account was to add a horrified witness.

Similar forms of treatment occurred on the Central Powers' side. In Austria, for instance, one of the country's most prominent psychiatrists, Julius Wagner-Jauregg, promoted the use of faradization at the university hospital clinic where he presided in Vienna. Shortly after the war, the well-respected doctor was investigated on accusations that soldiers had been subjected to "electrical torture" at his clinic. The investigation was a spin-off from a larger commission that was formed to examine unlawful acts com-mitted by high-ranking military personnel. Wagner-Jauregg had actually been sitting as one of the commissioners when the torture accusations began appearing in a Social Democratic weekly newspaper, *Der Freie Soldat* (The free soldier).[33] Although the hearing ended with the doctor's com-plete exoneration, the investigation produced a remarkable public debate about the nature of war neurosis.

Apart from Wagner-Jauregg himself, the other chief voice in the debate was Sigmund Freud, who had been called to testify as an expert witness at the commission. Freud prepared a memorandum for the occasion—an astonishing document in itself—but perhaps even more remarkable are the transcripts of the proceedings that took place on October 14 and 16, 1920.[34] The hearing focused on testimony presented by Walter Kauders, the soldier who had made the accusation against Wagner-Jauregg and the clinic, and on whose medical case the hearing turned. Wagner-Jauregg de-fended his practice by suggesting Kauders was a malingerer. After a long discussion, the commissioners asked Professor Freud his opinion about Wagner-Jauregg's methods of treatment. In his reply, and indeed, through-out his participation in the hearing, Freud framed the problem in social terms:

There is some truth in saying the newspapers agitate in an ugly manner out of sensationalism, out of a feeling of vengefulness against the old system. But it is also true that we had a people's army, that men were forced into military service, that they were not asked whether they liked to go to war, and that is why one has to understand people wanted to flee. The physicians had to play a role somewhat like that of a machine gun behind the front line, driving back those who fled. Certainly, this was the intent of the war administration. . . . There may have been some physicians who forgot their humanitarian duties and responded to the pressures put upon them in an elastic manner. They allowed their sense of power to make an appearance in a brutal fashion.[35]

In Freud's mind, the war forced doctors into an impossible compromise: rather than be guided by "the claims of humanity," the pressure of a national war meant treatment was bent toward the aim of restoring patients' fitness for service—turning citizens into "useful soldiers," as Yealland had phrased it. Freud admitted that the use of electric shock worked for this purpose, but only because it was painful—it made neurosis even more unpleasant than military service. "The practice," he flatly stated, "is too cruel."[36]

Freud managed to publicly support Wagner-Juaregg (but declined to vouch for the other clinic doctors) and yet still found ways to express his disagreement about his colleague's method of treatment. When there was occasion, he made careful mention of those medical doctors who adopted psychoanalytic techniques with "extraordinary therapeutic successes." He described a recent Psychoanalytic Congress in which plans were made to deploy psychoanalytic stations to treat war neurosis closer to the front— plans that were brought to a halt only with the collapse of the Central Powers.[37] In this respect, the war had an expansive effect on psychoanalytic practice and, in turn, on Freud's thinking. From this point forward, it was anxiety (or *Angst*) that would became the dominant force in Freud's model of the human psyche. His encounter with the commission gave him a new public platform to express his sense of the depth and complexity of psychic life. Against Wagner's mechanized conception of the mind, Freud insisted, over and over again, on the dynamic nature of the psyche: "We have to keep in mind," he declared at one point during the commission, that "there is a big difference between conscious refusal and unconscious refusal."[38] For Freud, the war neurotics' symptoms were profound evidence that war can also break out *within* the domain of the mind, indeed, that such devastating social conflicts also inflicted their damages at the level of the soul.

Defense by Representation

Fortunately for Wilfred Owen, the medical officers at Craiglockhart War Hospital for Neurasthenic Officers were not enamored by the disciplining power of electric current. Owen was assigned to Dr. Arthur J. Brock, a Scottish civilian doctor who had been temporarily conscripted into the Royal Army Medical Corps. At their first meeting in June 1917, Owen was still nervy, with an occasional stammer in his otherwise warm, deep voice. Brock, on the other hand, was described as "very tall, thin, hunched up shoulders, big blue hands, very chilly looking, with a long peaked nose that should have had a drip at the end of it."[39] Despite the differences—or perhaps because of them—the transference between patient and doctor was lively. Brock was deeply influenced by Galen's philosophical approach to medicine and emphasized a holistic treatment. He collected and translated many of the ancient medical texts and was part of the early twentieth-century humanist revival within medicine. For the Scottish doctor, neurasthenia was best understood as a profound disturbance between the individual and the environment.

Brock's relationship to psychoanalysis was ambivalent, although he published a paper in 1918 in which he promoted his view—like Freud's— that shell shock involved an unconscious malingering: "Here although the patient *refuses to acknowledge it to himself,* his whole being revolts against having to go back to the horrors from which he has been released." The disabling symptoms were proof enough that this repressed idea exists "at the back of his mind." For Brock, war neurasthenia represented a profoundly altered psychological state in which the whole life-impulse of the individual has come under the sway of "frightful war conditions" that leave "the soul of the patient in a state of general fearfulness."[40] Similar to Freud, the doctor understood the physical symptoms—the stammering, nightmares, tics, and disturbances of gait—to be outward expressions of an underlying illness of the soul. Focusing on physical symptoms would not mend the underlying psychic condition. Where Brock departed from psychoanalysis was in his method of treatment. The Scot advocated a more energetic approach, which he called "ergotherapy": a kind of work-cure

Portrait of Dr. Arthur J. Brock by unknown photographer. Copyright the English Faculty Library, University of Oxford and The Wilfred Owen Literary Estate.

that involved assigning patients various tasks designed to reintegrate them into their milieu.[41] One of Wilfred Owen's first assignments, for instance, was to tour a local foundry and then hammer out a copper bowl.

Apart from being a proponent of strenuous activity, Dr. Brock also assigned inward-looking exercises. Owen's next task was to write a poem about the ancient myth of Antaeus, a half giant who was invincible as long as he stayed in contact with the earth, his mother, Gaia. Hercules managed to defeat the giant by lifting him into the air, breaking his contact with the earth, where he could crush him in a bear hug. Antaeus was one of Brock's favorite symbols and served as the emblem of his theory; a picture of the wrestlers hung above his desk.[42] Although Brock did not describe it this way, the central action of the myth turns on the attachment to the maternal body.

Not long after the war, Brock published an extended account of his method of treatment in a book called *Health and Conduct.* Owen's work is mentioned briefly. Published in 1923, the book can be remembered as one of the first critical commentaries on the poet's work. Brock observed the decorum of patient confidentially, refraining from mentioning the fact that he treated Owen, but he would, of course, have had intimate knowl-edge of the experiences that provided fodder for the writer. Tellingly, the doctor chose to draw attention to Owen's use of dream-life: "In the power-ful war-poems of Wilfred Owen we read the heroic testimony of one who having in the most literal sense 'faced the phantoms of the mind' had *all but* laid them ere the last call came; they still appear in his poetry but he fears them no longer."[43]

Owen said little about his dreams in his letters, but it seems clear from the content of his poems that he was barraged by violent nightmares while at Craiglockhart (if not before). Moreover, his style and structure changed dramatically once Brock encouraged him to begin working directly with these haunting visions. The striking scene presented in "Dulce et Deco-rum Est," for instance, is almost certainly drawn from an incident when Owen's platoon was surprised by a gas attack on the night of April 6, 1917, (shortly before the railway embankment incident).

The first stanza of the poem lulls the reader with its languid descrip-tion of a weary battalion trudging toward some distant rest: "Men marched asleep. Many had lost their boots / But limped on, blood-shod ... Drunk with fatigue ..." This lethargy comes to an abrupt end in the second stanza:

"Gas! Gas! Quick boys!—An ecstasy of fumbling,
fitting the clumsy helmets just in time;
But someone still was yelling out and stumbling
And flound'ring like a man in fire or lime . . .
Dim, through the misty panes and thick green light,
As under a green sea, I saw him drowning.

In all my dreams, before my helpless sight,
He plunges at me, guttering, choking, drowning.

If in some smothering dreams you too could pace
Behind the wagon we flung him in,
And watch the white eyes writhing in his face,
His hanging face, like a devil's sick of sin;
If you could hear, at every jolt, the blood
Come gargling from the froth-corrupted lungs,
Obscene as cancer, bitter as the cud
Of vile, incurable sores on innocent tongues,
My friend, you would not tell with such high zest
To children ardent for some desperate glory,
The old Lie: Dulce et decorum est
Pro patria mori.[44]

Owen separates out the two middle lines of the poem, not quite breaking
the formal sonnet structure, but adding extra line breaks to emphasize and
distinguish this moment of terror. The last stanza manages to maintain the
concurrency of the experience, but begins to address the reader directly,
describing the death throes of the gassed man in the charged tones of an
eyewitness. Readers are transformed into an onlooker, if not quite a fellow
soldier in the beleaguered company. The increasingly impassioned testimony builds to the final lines of the poem, gathering a case against "the old
Lie." The Latin phrase is taken from Horace: "It is sweet and fitting to die
for one's country." Owen's ironic turn on the expression is often understood as a bitter indictment of the patriotic fervor that had gripped civilians at home.

An early draft of Owen's poem is dedicated "To Jessie Pope," a dedication
he canceled out and then wrote, "To a certain Poetess." Jessie Pope was a

Dulce et Decorum est.   318
[To a certain Poetess]

Bent double, like old beggars under sacks,
Knock-kneed, coughing like hags, we cursed through sludge,
Till on the clawing flares we turned our backs,
And towards our distant rest began to trudge,
Dragging the worst amongst us
~~Helping the worst amongst us~~, who'd no boots
But limped on, blood-shod. All went lame; ~~half~~ all blind;
Drunk with fatigue; deaf even to the hoots
Of tired, outstripped ~~f f~~ five-nines that dropped behind.

Then somewhere near in front: Whew... fup... fop... fup...
Gas shells or duds? We loosened masks in case —
And listened... Nothing... Far rumouring of Krupp...
Then ~~sudden~~ smartly, poison hit us in the face.
Gas! GAS! Quick boys! – And ecstasy of fumbling,
Fitting the clumsy helmets, just in time;
But someone still was yelling out, and stumbling,
And floundering like a man in fire or lime.

Dim, through the misty panes and heavy light,
As under a dark sea, I saw him drowning.
In all my dreams, before my helpless sight
He lunges at me, guttering, choking, drowning.

In all your dreams of you could slowly pace
Behind the limber that we flung him in,
And watch the white eyes turning in his face,
His hanging face, like a devil's dead of sin;
If you could hear at every jolt, the blood
Come gargling thick and frothy from the lung;
And think how once his face was like a bud,
Fresh as a country rose, and keen, and young,
You'd not go telling with such noble zest,
To small boys, ardent for some desperate glory,
The old lie; Dulce et decorum est
Pro patria mori.

                              Wilfred Owen.

virulently patriotic English poet and regular contributor to *Punch* and the
Daily Mail. She tirelessly promoted the Order of the White Feather—the
dramatic campaign that sought to shame men into enlisting. Pope recruited
women to hand white feathers to men who were not in uniform in public, a gesture that was designed to symbolically mark them as cowards.
Owen's poem seems to target Pope, serving as a kind of rebuttal to her
blind nationalism. In response to her campaign, Owen provides a horrify-
ingly graphic account of a gas attack, as if to shake the activist out of her
"high zest."

But in fact, Owen sent his "gas poem" to his mother. He had begun
sending her his new experiments writing about the war, what he called his
"trench sketches," as enclosures in his letters from Craiglockhart throughout the fall of 1917. At the end of September he sent her a version of "The
Sentry" with explicit instructions not to show it to anyone. Two weeks
later came "Dulce et Decorum Est," which he noted "is not private, but not
final."[45] Although his letters remain warm, insisting on the "unconfinable
sympathy" between them, the inclusion of these violent poems tenders a
more ambiguous message, a kind of oblique allegation. Indeed, the revised
dedication suggests that his reproach has multiple (female) addressees,
including his mother, who also fails to see the horrors soldiers were facing at
the front.[46] Leaving open this question of audience might allow for a more
modest reading of the poem, one that privileges the narrator's poignant
sense of vulnerability rather than indiscriminate moral outrage. "Dulce et
Decorum Est" teeters on its centerpiece image of the "choking, guttering,
drowning" man, a vision that fixates the narrator, indeed, which seems to
hold him in a perpetual bondage, leaving him helpless to control or mod-
erate its affective charge.

Owen was not, of course, the only one to be held hostage by such
images. Variations of this scene reappear in any number of works about
the war, including in illustrations of the journal the soldiers themselves
produced at Craiglockhart. On the Central Powers side, the German artist
Otto Dix published a portfolio of fifty etchings simply titled *Der Krieg*
(The war). Amongst the grisly catalog are two pictures that could have
served as illustrations for Owen's poem: "Sturmtruppe geht unter Gas vor"
(Shock troops advance under gas attack) and "Verwundeter (Herbst 1916,
Bapaume)" (Wounded man [autumn 1916, Bapaume]). The combination
of eerie flashbulb lighting and plain, descriptive captioning suggests Dix
witnessed these scenes directly. Despite the almost childlike rendering of

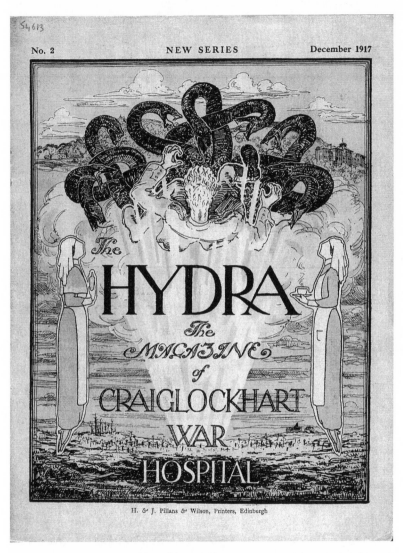

No. 2   NEW SERIES   December 1917

The
HYDRA
The MAGAZINE of
CRAIGLOCKHART
WAR
HOSPITAL

H. & J. Pillans & Wilson, Printers, Edinburgh

Cover of the Hydra: The Magazine of Craiglockhart War Hospital, *no. 2, new series (December 1917). Illustration by Lieutenant Adrian Berrington. Copyright the English Faculty Library, University of Oxford and The Wilfred Owen Literary Estate.*

Lieutenant Adrian Berrington, "Shell Shock!" Interior illustration from the Hydra: The
Magazine of Craiglockhart War Hospital, *no. 2, new series (December 1917). Copyright
the English Faculty Library, University of Oxford and The Wilfred Owen Literary Estate.*

the figures (or perhaps because of this), one gets the sense that these representations depict actual incidents. Like Owen's poem, the spectator is
positioned as a direct onlooker to a nightmarish event. Engaging the series
as a whole, one gets the sense of having wandered directly into the artist's
nightmare, a ghastly landscape complete with a voice that quietly accuses,
"Can't you see?" Viewers of Dix's images are granted even less distance than
Owen affords his readers by way of his ironic conclusion. There is almost

Otto Dix, "Sturmtruppe geht unter Gas vor" (Storm troops advance under gas attack), from the portfolio Der Krieg *(The war), 1924. Etching, aquatint, and drypoint; plate 7⅝ × 11 ⁵⁄₁₆ inches (19.3 × 28.8 cm). Published by Karl Nierendorf, Berlin. Printed by Otto Felsing, Berlin. Gift of Abby Aldrich Rockefeller. Copyright The Museum of Modern Art. Licensed by SCALA / Art Resource, NY. Copyright Estate of Otto Dix / SODRAC (2016).*

no sense of a narrative shield here. The shock troops' advance is terrifyingly proximate; the wounded man is caught forever in his death throes, perpetually clutching at his chest with his hanging face, blood gargling up from froth-corrupted lungs.

Being held in perpetual bondage to an image is precisely how Freud defined trauma in 1920, when he wrote *Beyond the Pleasure Principle*, based, in part, on his reflections on the symptoms of war neurotics: "dreams occurring in traumatic neuroses have the characteristic of repeatedly bringing the patient back into the situation of his accident, a situation from which he wakes up in another fright.... The patient is, as one might say, *fixated* on his trauma."[47] Freud proposes that the undistorted return to the situation of the fright in dream-life—what he called "the compulsion to repeat"—provides a means for the mind to gain mastery over an experience that was overwhelming at the time of its initial occurrence. In such instances, a portion of reality escaped the individual's perception, even as

Otto Dix, "Verwundeter (Herbst 1916, Bapaume)" (Wounded man [autumn 1916, Bapaume]), from the portfolio Der Krieg *(The war), 1924. Etching and aquatint, 7 ¾ × 11 ⁷⁄₁₆ inches (19.7 × 29 cm). Published by Karl Nierendorf, Berlin. Printed by Otto Felsing, Berlin. Gift of Abby Aldrich Rockefeller. Copyright The Museum of Modern Art. Licensed by SCALA / Art Resource, NY. Copyright Estate of Otto Dix / SODRAC (2016).*

it made its impress felt at another level. Freud surmises that compulsive dreams help to bind the destructive force of this "missed" experience retrospectively. Returning to the fright over and over gradually transforms the dreamer into an *active* agent of a situation that he initially experienced *passively.* In such cases, normal human functioning becomes twisted toward a need for mastery—the subject is driven less by pleasure seeking than by a need to gain control of the experience. Dix's choice of medium is telling in this respect—printmaking serves the impulse to "compulsively repeat" an image. Like the traumatic dream, the process mechanically produces a proliferation of (seemingly) exact copies, as if one could tame and contain the experience within the confines of a frame.

Is it any wonder that Dix's series did not sell? As with Owen's work, the artist's unbleached presentation of these terrors was rejected by most of the populace and especially by ex-servicemen whose heroic legacy it seemed to challenge directly. Eventually Dix would become a target in the Nazis' purge of "degenerate art." Immediately after the Great War, it was tales of courage that were wanted, indeed, demanded, not the self-pitying complaints of cowards. This dimension of human vulnerability—the awful "fearfulness of soul" that this war begot—was found to be unbearable in the immediate aftermath of the war.

"These Days, Who Still Has a Soul?"

What of the fear that our own wars have begot? Much ink has been spilled about our current geopolitical landscapes of terror including an important body of scholarship that attempts to intervene in the political uses of fear. While this deep mapping is indispensable to our capacity to critique the social and political dimensions of violence, it is striking how few scholars are willing to consider the ways fear grips and dispossesses people at more intimate levels of existence, how this emotion necessarily manifests in the bodies of specific persons. Instead of the "fearfulness of soul" that doctors at Craiglockhart attempted to grasp and ameliorate at the individual level, the catchphrase of current inquiry is "the politics of fear"— a slogan that would seem to posit a landscape utterly bereft of a human population. Perhaps like so much of twenty-first-century life, fear has itself become something impersonal. Or perhaps our contemporary discourse has become infected with the very anxiety it seeks to dispel—perhaps we, too, flee from any intimate encounters with the psychic damage that our wars have begot.

Among the contemporary Wars on Terror, only once did I catch sight of something that resembled the "fearfulness of soul" that made its impress felt so broadly during the Great War. It was after Seymour Hersh broke the story about the prisoner abuse Abu Ghraib, after those flat, horizonless photographs of torture began to populate newspapers and magazines and Internet websites. Indeed, it was just about the time the awful images had finally begun to fade from public view that Philip Gourevitch and Errol Morris published a story in the *New Yorker* about Sabrina Harman, "the woman behind the camera at Abu Ghraib."[48] In fact, the twenty-six-year-old army specialist was just as often positioned in front of the camera as behind it, perhaps most famously, caught posing with a big smile and thumbs-up sign in front of a corpse topped with ice in plastic bags and lying on a black rubber body bag. The article offers a complex, ambiguous portrait of the young woman and of life at Abu Ghraib. Like many reservists, Harman joined the army to help pay for college. She experienced Iraq as something unreal, as she put it, "like a dream."

In fact, Harman did report a dream in a letter she wrote home to the woman she called her wife. It was written on her first night at the prison. She describes her arrival to Abu Ghraib and seeing two helicopters poised to take prisoners off:

> I'm scared of the helicopters because of the dream. I think I wrote it down before. I saw a helicopter and it looked like the tail was swaying back and forth then it did it again then a huge flame/round shot up and it exploded. I turned around and we were under attack, I didn't have my weapon (gun) so all we could do was hide under these picknick tables. So back to the prison . . . we get to our buildings and I step out of my truck right in front of a picknick table.—I almost freaked out. I have a bad feeling about this place. I want to leave as soon as possible! We are still hoping to be home X-mas or soon after.—
> I love you.
> I am going to go get some sleep.
> I'll write you again soon.
> Please don't give up on me![49]

After reading this account I found myself turning away from the *New Yorker* article for a time. I suspect it was something about Harman's shockingly simple account of being afraid, something about the silly misspellings, the intimacy the letter conveyed that generated an uncomfortable mix of pity and aversion.

Harman's fellow officers also found her kindly and naive: "She was just too nice to be a soldier," her team leader reported. It was clear Harman was not leadership material, nor was she a particularly good follower. She liked to look. She had the inclinations of a taxidermist; dead things fascinated her and she took many pictures of life in this inanimate state. At Abu Ghraib, she felt herself growing numb. She had no responsibility for what happened on the military intelligence block where most of the abuses took place. But for complex, ambiguous reasons, she began photographing the prisoners whom she encountered in Tier 1A, who were naked, handcuffed to the bars of their cells, stretched over a bunk bed, or in other age-old torture positions. It is the deep ambiguity of her actions and state of mind that Gourevitch and Morris seize upon, the way she ricocheted from "childish mockery to casual swagger to sympathy to cruelty to titillation to self-justification to self-doubt to outrage to identification to despair." Throughout this tumult she somehow came to use her camera as a means to excise herself from the torture that she witnessed. Many of her now infamous images, Gourevitch and Morris ultimately claim, are compelling not because they show "the human form laid bare and reduced to raw matter" but rather because they present an "original image of inhumanity that admits no immediately self-evident reading." Their enduring fascination resides in their "mystery and inscrutability—in all that is concealed by all that it reveals."

This gossamer description could be mistaken for a page from Freud's *Interpretation of Dreams.* Gourevitch and Morris might well be musing about what kinds of representational acts, and in which logical variations, constitute the human soul. And is it so strange—in the midst of the stifling fog of war, when the difference between reality and dream become hard to distinguish—that photography would offer itself up as a venue to work through the most inscrutable of experiences? In the voluminous discussion of the Abu Ghraib prison photographs, among the many claims and demands made on their behalf, I do not think anyone has dared to figure them as sites where a young American reservist struggled to preserve her soul, as a coarse and crude articulation of "the truth untold / The pity of war, the pity war distilled."[50] We no longer have reverence or even patience for the inexorably conflicted voice of one who is both a participant in and observer of the evils of total war. Our generation has undoubtedly judged Harman and found her testimony to contain little more than the self-pitying complaints of a coward. Perhaps we will have to wait for the next generation's judgment to see if this young woman's wretched disclosure also bears something that could be called courage.

CHAPTER 4

The Artist's Defense

The City in Ruins Dream

Since wars begin in the minds of men, it is in the minds of men that the defences of peace must be constructed.

—Preamble to the Constitution of the United Nations Educational, Scientific, and Cultural Organization

"THERE IS SOMETHING UNREAL about this air war over Britain," Edward R. Murrow calmly remarks during one of his radio broadcasts in the early days of the London Blitz. "Much of it you can't see, but the aircraft are up in the clouds, out of sight."[1] Murrow's struggle to convey this experience that has passed beyond human scale is one of the hallmarks of the American journalist's work from this period. A month into the nightly bombings, for example, he describes the "freakish" nature of the damage inflicted by the unseen German planes: "A bomb may explode at an intersection and the blast will travel down two streets, shattering windows for a considerable distance, while big windows within a few yards of the bomb crater remain intact." He adds, in his characteristically neutral tone, that the glass "generally falls into the street, rather than be blown inwards." One of these broadcasts was delivered from the mouth of an air raid shelter near Trafalgar Square while sirens wail in the background. Another was recorded in whispered tones because "three or four people are sleeping on mattresses on the floor" of Murrow's studio.[2]

The journalist mesmerized radio listeners back home with his detailed daily accounts of the air war being waged across the Atlantic. The broadcasts did more than simply offer headline news to American audiences. They also attempted to convey what life felt like in the city under siege: the unassuming bravery of ordinary citizens, new pressures brought by the war measures, the eerie silence left in the streets after the evacuation of the children, the way the British class system found a new venue of expression in the nightlife of bomb shelters.

But as the Blitz stretched into weeks and then into months, Murrow became more and more preoccupied with imparting what he called the war's "unreality." The air war pushed the broadcaster's powers of description to the limit. On September 20, 1940, he delivered one of his most surreal accounts. As usual, the evening radio program was broadcast to Americans from the middle of England's night, in this case, at three thirty in the morning London time:

> The scale of this air war is so great the reporting of it is not easy. . . .
> We've read you the communiqués and tried to give you an honest
> estimate of the wounds inflicted upon this, the best bombing target
> in the world. But the business of living and working in this city is
> very personal—the little incidents, the things the mind retains, are
> in themselves unimportant, but they somehow weld together to
> form the hard core of memories that will remain when the last "all
> clear" has sounded. That's why I want to talk for just three or four
> minutes about the things we haven't talked about before; for many
> of these impressions it is necessary to reach back through only one
> long week. . . . One night I stood in front of a smashed grocery
> store and heard dripping inside. It was the only sound in all
> London. Two cans of peaches had been drilled clean through by
> flying glass and the juice was dripping down onto the floor.
>   There was a flower shop in the East End. Nearly every other
> building in the block had been smashed. There was a funeral
> wreath in the window of the shop—price: three shillings and six
> pence, less than a dollar. In front of Buckingham Palace there's a
> bed of red and white flowers—untouched—the reddest flowers
> I've ever seen.[3]

It is difficult to grasp the extra-ordinariness of these eventide impressions. After months of straightforward, realist coverage, the most potent means to convey the "unreality" of the Blitz arrived in the sound of dripping peach juice, the sight of a funeral wreath in a shop window, and mesmerizingly red flowers in the Palace gardens. Perhaps the best that can be said of this strange, composite picture of London circa September 1940 is that after weeks of terrifying night raids, Murrow found himself in the middle of a dream.

Murrow's determined attempt to grasp, indeed, to picture that which was occurring around him makes these radio broadcasts one of the more remarkable records of civilian experience of air war. They testify to one of the most disquieting ideas to emerge during this period of human history: a belief that the most effective way of waging war involved the obliteration of civilian life through air attack. Although the fantasy of Total War had existed for centuries (its seeds having been sown during the Napoleonic Wars), this particular doctrine took on new potency in the 1930s with the development of aerial bombardment technology. As the Italian general and theorist of air power Giulio Douhet realized, "aeroplanes" would utterly transform the future of war by transforming the location of the front. The technical evolution effectively erased the distinction between soldiers and civilians: "Nothing man can do on the surface of the earth can interfere with a plane in flight, moving freely in the third dimension."[4] And of life on the ground, Walter Benjamin would lament: "A generation that had gone to school on horse drawn street cars now stood under the open sky in a landscape where nothing remained unchanged but the clouds and, beneath those clouds, in the field of force of destructive torrents and explosions, the tiny fragile, human body."[5]

The new terrors from above had a particularly devastating effect on the field of the aesthetic. In his Zurich lectures, "Air War and Literature," W. G. Sebald describes the perplexing literary silence surrounding the destruction of German cities and towns in the latter half of the Second World War. Some six hundred thousand German civilians were killed by Allied air raids—ten times that of British civilian casualties—and another seven and half million people were left homeless. German cities themselves suffered unparalleled physical destruction. And yet, as Sebald notes, there was a "tacit agreement, equally binding on everyone, that the true state of material and moral ruin in which the country found itself was *not to be described.*" The destruction of the German cities—a destruction that was experienced by the great majority of the population—remained, Sebald marvels, "under a kind of taboo like a shameful family secret, a secret that perhaps could not even be privately acknowledged."[6] The destruction wrought from above was therefore both unimaginable and unspeakable. This air war transfigured the dimensions of the battlefield and simultaneously shattered the human capacity to communicate. It left its victims bereft of that which seems most inalienable, ruining the securest among our human possessions: the ability to convey lived experience.

In light of this profound wounding, I suspect the primary target of air war—indeed, perhaps of all violence—is the human mind. This hypothesis repositions air war's manifest threat to bodies and the built environment as, in fact, a radical attack upon the psyche—and more specifically, an attempt to destroy the human being's capacity to freely assign meaning to experience. This is evidenced, as Sebald observes, by the fact that literature numbered among the casualties in Britain's air war on Germany. This new form of violence ravaged one of the established means for creating and sharing experience.

While literature fell, other aesthetic forms arose in response. Perhaps akin to the way resistance assumes myriad forms depending on who and what is being fought against, the artistic community found new venues of expression. In particular during this period, photography emerged as one of the chief styluses for recording what could not be written otherwise. In the early years of air war, this medium became one of the most potent tools for communicating the new landscapes of emotional life, the new states of mind created by this terrible force that targeted civilian life and yet effectively remained "out of sight." In response to this aggressive attack on the mind, photography offered a special kind of defense-by-representation. Photographic film provides a sensitive surface capable of registering perceptual traces and impressions. These impressions, in turn, can be developed into images endowed with an illusory reality that can help fill the holes that this form of political violence attempts to rip in the fabric of human experience. In this early era of air war, photography became one of the civilian's best defenses.

This chapter considers Lee Miller's photographs of the Blitz as an exemplary instance in which photography functioned like a species of dream. That is to say, for Miller, the medium provided the scaffolding for a symbolic *form* of thinking in which the damage caused by air war could be re-presented in an effort to discharge its destructive force. This approach to Miller's work leans on two, interrelated insights. The first is Freud's own reliance on the work of art as a model for his concept of dream-work. Freud was fascinated by art. His English editor, James Strachey, lists some twenty-two papers in which Freud dealt directly or indirectly with artists' individual works, themes in literature, or general problems of artistic creativity. Throughout these papers, Freud treated art as a model for unconscious psychic process. The artist's capacity to symbolically play with day residues finds an everyday parallel in the processes of dream-work. What I aim to do in this chapter is show how dream-work, in turn, can be used to describe the psychological work—that is, the emotional digestion—

that aesthetic productions strive to achieve.[7] Photography, to borrow Virginia Woolf's phrasing, provided Miller with the means to "think peace into existence" in the midst of air war.[8]

The second insight is more specific. In the century since Freud introduced his method of dream analysis, theorists and analysts have elaborated on how the modality of visible images projected onto the dream screen possesses facilitating and defensive properties. More specifically, a dream is thought to provide a visual buffer that can double as a protective shield to traumatic overwhelming. As Didier Anzieu describes, dreams weave a new psychical skin that can reinforce an ego whose defenses are embattled or defective. Or in a more quotidian sense, the "film of the dream" does the nightly work of repairing the small ruptures in the skin ego that are implicit in daily functioning.[9] Such elaborations of dream theory lend a new, broader significance to oneiric life, and perhaps in particular in times of social or political crisis. These fragile visual membranes, so quick to break and dissipate, do the work of protecting the psyche from excitations coming from the external world that would threaten to destroy the mind with their intensity.

This more recent recognition of the dream's defensive function borrows its conceptualization, in part, from what Freud called the *Reizschutz*—a protective shield for the mind. In framing his theory of trauma in *Beyond the Pleasure Principle,* Freud conjured an image of a specialized apparatus that envelops the organism, filtering external stimuli that would otherwise overwhelm the delicate interior organs of the psyche.[10] One of the questions this chapter pursues is whether photography can also harbor this protective function. Can these images also provide a kind of *Reizschutz* for the mind? Freud himself provides reasons to make the connection between photography and dream. In *Die Traumdeutung* he makes a direct comparison between the psychical apparatus and optical instruments such as the camera. Indeed, this was one of his favorite metaphors that he returned to repeatedly, the last time in *Moses and Monotheism*. In this text, he notes that early experiences possess special significance because the child's psyche is not yet fully developed; early impressions are like "a photographic exposure which can be developed after any interval of time and transformed into a picture. . . . What children have experienced at the age of two and have not understood, need never be remembered by them except in dreams."[11] Photography, therefore, like dream, can be understood as a method for processing difficult stimuli. The camera filters external excitations, capturing information in small samples. This breaking down of the mass stimuli is usually followed by some kind of darkroom work in which the initial impressions are edited and developed into positive pictures. Like any metaphor, the comparison is not perfect. Photography perhaps fails to convey the conflictual character of the psyche; it cannot show the extent of the forces that have an interest in allowing or prohibiting certain images to enter consciousness. Despite the flaws in the analogy, photography remained one of Freud's favorite metaphors for psychical process.[12]

In less technical terms, my goal here is to explore how the photography of air war can help us think through the psychological dimensions of violence—both its destructive force and our capacity to resist it. As Julia Kristeva has forcefully argued, it is the imaginary dimension that provides the ultimate shield from attacks on our being—both from psychological and biological traumas and from external forms of social and political aggression: "The imaginary," she suggests, metabolizes these attacks, "transforms them, sublimates them, works-through them and in this way keeps us alive."[13] Kristeva is referring to fantasies and dreams as well as to aesthetic forms such as literature.[14] In this chapter, this imaginary landscape is expanded to include photography and, more specifically, those who wielded this medium as a means of civil defense in the early days of air war.

This past moment has become significant again, not least because the idea of obliterating a civilian population via the "third dimension" has reached new heights in the twenty-first century. The contemporary era of air war was perhaps inaugurated on September 11, 2001, when airplanes became the bomb *and* the front, when the indiscriminate destruction of civilian life could itself occur "up in the clouds, out of sight," as Edward Murrow might have said. The period since the 9/11 attacks has been one of constant air war: apart from the NATO-led campaigns in Afghanistan, the United States has launched thousands of unmanned air strikes in Pakistan and Yemen. Drones hover twenty-four hours a day over several parts of these countries, striking homes, vehicles, and public spaces without warning. In direct violation of the Geneva Conventions, their presence terrorizes the local civilian populations.[15] The Syrian civil war has added another (and at the time of writing, unfinished) chapter to this new era of air war.

While potent evidence has been gathered about the particular kinds of damage air war inflicts, relatively less attention has been paid to our collective and individual strategies of defense—the tools and methods a civilian population has at its disposal to represent and shield itself from this form of terror.[16] The lessons learned at the dawn of air war are perhaps relevant again.

The Guardians of Sleep

The first substantial expression of modern air war occurred when the German Luftwaffe's Condor Legion—under direct orders from Lieutenant Colonel Wolfram von Richthofen and assisted by a few Italian planes—bombed a small Basque town in northern Spain late in the day on April 26, 1937. The market town of Guernica provided a prime target for Germany to test out its new air war capabilities. This preliminary military exercise helped the Nazis develop their *Blitzkrieg* tactic. In addition to the incendiary bombs that ravaged the town's center, machine guns took fleeing civilians as their target. Remarkably, news of the attack reached international audiences almost immediately. The *Times* of London carried a front-page report by George Steer on April 27, and photographers were immediately dispatched to capture images of the destruction. One of these pictures even managed to capture flames still licking through the remains of Guernica's streets. On April 28, photographs of dead women and children were published in the Communist paper *L'Humanitié.* By April 30, the images of the bombed-out town appeared in a variety of Parisian papers, including *Le Figaro* and *Ce Soir,* which Pablo Picasso was known to have read. His first sketches for his famous *Guernica* mural date from the first of May.[17]

In an antiwar essay written during the time, Virginia Woolf describes receiving a package of these pictures in the morning's post. She reports that one photograph shows dead children. Another shows a section of a house: "A bomb has torn open the side; there is still a bird-cage hanging in what was presumably the sitting-room, but the rest of the house looks like nothing so much as a bunch of spillikins suspended in mid-air." When Woolf looks at these pictures, her feelings become unequivocal: "some fusion takes place within us; however different the education, the traditions behind us, our sensations are the same . . . the same words rise to our lips. War is an abomination; a barbarity; war must be stopped."[18] As they did for Picasso, the photographs of Guernica aroused potent feelings in Woolf, giving rise to an inner sense of conviction from which her unequivocal voice found strength.[19]

Guernica, bombed by the German Condor Legion, 1937 (unknown photographer).
Imagno/Hulton Archive/Getty Images.

One could read such aesthetic encounters as exemplars of what Jacques Rancière calls the "redistribution of the sensible," that is, new organizations of the sensory world that reconfigure the landscape of what can be seen and thought.[20] If air war wreaked damage from "the third dimension," photography was called upon to combat this violence through its networks of distribution, its capacity to generate an international alignment of witnesses, to offer a venue for the world spectator's shock, censure, and grief. There is much to be said, in other words, about the relation between the new violence rained down from above and photography's ability to help weave a new community of aesthetic judgment—a *sensus communis*—below.

But beyond journalistic exposé, photography also served as a special instrument for describing the *inward* effect of the outward destruction brought about by air war. In this respect, Edward Murrow was not alone in his presentation of the London Blitz as a dreamscape. Photographer, lapsed surrealist, and former *Vogue* cover girl, Lee Miller, similarly turned up in London on the eve of this "People's War" and she too was captivated by and sought to capture the city's "unreal reality."

Miller landed in London in June 1939 to join her lover, the painter and surrealist promoter Roland Penrose. By the end of the summer the pair were visiting Picasso in France, returning to England once news that Hitler had invaded Poland broke at the beginning of September. They arrived back in London just in time to hear the first air raid sirens and watch the enormous gray, antiaircraft balloons rise into the sky. It would be another year, however, before Hitler's blitzkrieg reached English shores. The Führer authorized an all-out assault on the British capital beginning on September 6, 1940. London was bombed for seventy-six consecutive nights. By the end of May 1941, some forty-three thousand civilians, half of them Londoners, had been killed in one of the longest city sieges in modern times.

As an American, Lee Miller was prevented from joining the thousands of women who enlisted in the auxiliary forces, so she kept busy working as a staff photographer for British *Vogue* magazine. Already an established commercial photographer, the Blitz returned Miller to her surrealist sensibilities, cultivated years earlier by a Paris circle that included Man Ray, Paul Éluard, and Jean Cocteau. During the war, Miller made a daily trek between her home near Hampstead Heath in north London and *Vogue*'s Bond Street offices in the West End, wending through the London streets and recording the most arresting sights exposed by the night's bombings. Her pictures, like Murrow's reports, took cognizance of the way the cityscape was arranged and rearranged each night like so much dream furniture.

Some of the photographer's images found their way into the public sphere in 1941, when, together with several dozen other British press photographs, they appeared in a slim book called *Grim Glory: Pictures of Britain under Fire* (published in the United States under the title *Bloody but Unbowed*; a smaller group was also published in British *Vogue* in 1941). Designed to complement Murrow's broadcasts—he also wrote a brief preface—the book was a deliberate propaganda effort aimed at shifting U.S. sentiment toward intervention. As the publishers' write in their foreword, the book is "the expression of a feeling." More specifically, it attempts to convey the "heroic, exasperated, resolute, muddle-headed, defiant, insensitive—in a word, *English*—behaviour of ordinary people under the most prolonged intensive battering ever inflicted on civilians."[21] But like Murrow's radio broadcasts, Miller's contributions to this book are more preoccupied with conveying the surprising *unreality* of the bombings. This is to say, her pictures are less interested in transmitting a heroic English mentality than in capturing the uncanny laws of blast. Perhaps because of their outsider status—both were Americans—Miller and Murrow remained relatively abreast of the widespread efforts to manufacture national sentiment. Rather like the dreamer who struggles to find a way to describe the foreign territory of the dream, Miller and Murrow occupied the position of outside recorders, transcribing the strange unreality in which they found themselves immersed. Indeed, both in their own ways took on the central function Freud gave to dreams—guardians of sleep. As Londoners grew more and more fearful of the terrors night might bring, Miller and Murrow generated more and more fantastic images, both verbal and pictorial, pressing the day residues through fantasy operations in a way that attempted to give expression to the emotional needs and desires of the civilian population.

Dotted throughout *Grim Glory*, Miller's pictures dominate a section of the book called "The Ironies of War." There is a brief textual introduction to the section: "If all that one saw was unrelieved tragedy life would be unendurable in these besieged cities. Fortunately, the wanton behaviour of explosives and blast occasionally produces effects that are ironical, freakish, beautiful and sometimes even funny, although the irony is grim and the humour threaded through with pathos."[22] The dozen or so pictures in this section mobilize all these literary tricks and add something more. Miller has a gifted eye for capturing composites; indeed, she armed herself

with all the techniques of dream-work: displacement, condensation, symbolization, and secondary revision. Through her lens, for instance, a half-
blown-up building in Knightsbridge becomes a metonym of the Venetian
Bridge of Sighs. One can imagine floating along the Rio di Palazzo in a
gondola under this famous arch. In another, Miller pictures the door of
a church that is spewing bricks from its innards, as if the entranceway had

Lee Miller, "Bridge of Sighs," Lowndes Street, Knightsbridge, London, England, 1940.
Copyright Lee Miller Archives, England, 2016. All rights reserved. www.leemiller.co.uk.

been caught mid-regurgitation. Through an inspired use of captioning, the menacing sight is transfigured into a Nonconformist chapel. The dazzling interplay of visual and linguistic symbolic forms transforms the spectator's view of these chaotic ruins into an organized agitation for religious liberty.

On the same roll of film, Miller pulled back to capture a long shot of the same scene. Here the vomiting doorway is viewed awry, and all that remains of the larger building are several enormous pillars. Miller's caption reads like one of Julia Child's recipes: "1 Nonconformist Chapel + 1 bomb = Greek Temple." The composition calls for a new thesis about the end of empire, or perhaps the potent survival and return of antiquity, or

Lee Miller, "Nonconformist Chapel," London, England, 1940. Copyright Lee Miller Archives, England, 2016. All rights reserved. www.leemiller.co.uk.

perhaps the picture simply offers itself up as a site for contemplating the human fascination with ruins. If dreams represent desire fulfilled, here Miller remakes London into Venice and Athens. Through the imaginary mechanisms of dream-work, she impishly suggests that bombs can actually *add* cultural value and new tourist destinations to the city.

At times Miller shows off her quirky knowledge of art history, as in "Baroque Made Rococo." In this image a man in formal dress provides a scale for the massive, melted "rococo" candelabrum in the window. His smile, caught at the instant of its unfolding, acts like a guide for the spectator's own reaction, which is to say, we are invited to share in the joke. In a 1927 paper, Freud added to his early thesis on jokes, arguing that humor

Lee Miller, "1 Nonconformist Chapel + 1 bomb = Greek Temple," London, England, 1940.
Copyright Lee Miller Archives, England, 2016. All rights reserved. www.leemiller.co.uk.

Lee Miller, "Baroque Made Rococo," London, England, 1940. Copyright Lee Miller Archives, England, 2016. All rights reserved. www.leemiller.co.uk.

yields pleasure because it economizes affect. Where a situation might normally call for the expression of anger, frustration, pain, or terror, a good joke saves on this expenditure of feeling. Freud even risks a joke to illustrate: a criminal who is being led out to the gallows on a Monday remarks, "Well, the week's beginning nicely."[23] Humor liberates because it denies the arrows of reality; it refuses to submit to suffering and thereby preserves for us some measure of dignity. The gravest wounds of the world are lightened when they can become occasions for laughter.

Sometimes Miller's humor is angled deliberately toward her colleagues' gratification. Before they found their way into the book, Miller hung her pictures up on the walls of *Vogue*'s Bond Street offices. One can imagine her playfully inserting one of her photographs among the mock-ups for the next issue: "Fashion-note: Lamp-posts are worn cock-eyed this year in smart Belgravia." This is Miller's creative dream-thinking at its best: in her hands, a grotesquely twisted lamppost becomes delicate haute couture.

In another image, Miller provides visual illustration of Sebald's thesis about air war's effects on language. "Remington Silent" plays on the name

Lee Miller, "Lamp-Posts Are Worn Cock-Eyed in Belgravia This Year," London, England, 1940. Copyright Lee Miller Archives, England, 2016. All rights reserved. www.leemiller.co.uk.

Lee Miller, "Remington Silent," London, England, 1940. Copyright Lee Miller Archives, England, 2016. All rights reserved. www.leemiller.co.uk.

of a well-known typewriter of the time, but here its keys are mute. The pictorial image is called upon to stand in for the traditional means of signifying experience through words. And although photography is itself a silent medium, the image manages to testify to the way traditional means of communication were disabled by air war. As Miller's son, Antony Penrose, proposes, "The shattered machine taps out an eloquent essay on the war's assault on culture."[24] Miller mobilizes surrealism's penchant for found objects and ironic juxtaposition. As in dream, even ruined artifacts can take on a renewed meaning.

This surreal record of the London Blitz surely calls for pause. If we treat Miller's photographs and Murrow's broadcasts as historical testimony, one might be forced to reach a startling conclusion: one of the most pivotal political moments from the twentieth century was best captured and conveyed to distant audiences in terms of a dream. The Nazis' ideology presumed that their program of air war would compel Londoners to rise up and demand a new government, one that would make peace with Germany as so much of Europe had done.[25] And yet in this "People's War" the civilian's best defense against this brand of terrorism appeared to be dream-work. Surely this work raises new questions about the significance of this psychical process in relation to social and political aggression, about the profound importance of these interior, imaginary activities that can shield us from attacks on our being. If fascist regimes seek to "aestheticize political life," as Walter Benjamin famously proposed,[26] Miller's photographs and Murrow's radio broadcasts provide a model of civil resistance, showing us how dream-life can serve as one of our most important modes of defense.

The Politics of Reverie

Since the publication of *The Interpretation of Dreams*, the mysterious thoughts that come to us while we are asleep have been regarded as paradigmatic of the unconscious and central to any theory of mind. In his *New Introductory Lectures*, Freud reiterated that it was with the discovery of the laws that govern dreams, and specifically the dream-work, "that analysis took the step from being a psychotherapeutic procedure to being a depth psychology."[27] And while much of the classical theory of dream interpretation has remained intact, there have been numerous revisions and expansions over the years, including Freud's own grappling with "traumatic dreams" in *Beyond the Pleasure Principle*. This postwar text marks the first time Freud openly addressed the problem that some dreams seem "impossible to classify as wish fulfilments."[28] He initially regarded these two types of dream as independent, but Sándor Ferenczi extended and opened the latter view by defining every dream as "an attempt at a better mastery and settling of traumatic experiences, so to speak, in the sense of an *esprit d'escalier*."[29] Freud appeared to add his tacit agreement by suggesting that no one escapes the traumas of childhood experience that return to us in our dreams.[30] Infancy is a time of nameless dreads, and the predominance of visual imagery in dreams perhaps speaks clearest to the idea that their central purpose is to bind anxiety, or to use more contemporary terms, to work through otherwise unspeakable mental pain.

After Freud's death, dream theory has both extended this avenue and yet remained faithful to the early manual. Part of this evolution can be characterized as a shift of emphasis: from a focus on interpretation toward a renewed questioning of what sort of object a dream is and what psychical functions it serves. The work of two more recent thinkers of these questions, Wilfred Bion and Didier Anzieu, helps elucidate what Miller's and Murrow's representations of the London Blitz achieved, how their interventions into the imaginary provided a unique form of defense from the Nazis' attacks on civilian life by means of the instrument of air war.

British analyst Wilfred Bion, born just before the turn of the century, had his own particular intimacy with Total War, having served as a tank commander in France from 1917 to 1919. His *War Memoirs* are filled with accounts of being flattened to the ground by the force of exploding shells, warnings about the distance at which splinters can kill (eight hundred yards), and vivid descriptions such as an eerie valley filled with demolished tanks that bore gaping, blackened holes, a "terrible sight . . . too horrible to look at." Bion also recorded the crippling psychological effects of these experiences, which produced "nightmares out of which one started up suddenly with sweat pouring down one's face."[31] In this respect, the *Memoirs* graphically illustrate one of the most dangerous aspects of Total War—the way a subject can lose the capacity to "distinguish dream from reality":

> The tat-tat-tat of the German machine-guns would chime in with your dream with uncanny effect, so that when you awoke you wondered whether you were dreaming. The machine-gun made you think everything was genuine, and only by degrees you recovered yourself to fall into uneasy sleep again.
>
> It didn't take long for interest in life to die out. Soon I found myself almost hopeless. I used to lie on my back and stare at the low roof. Sometimes I stared for hours at a small piece of mud that hung from the roof by a grass and quivered to the explosion of the shells. . . . This may seem hardly possible to you. But the fact remains that life had now reached such a pitch that horrible mutilations or death could not conceivably be worse. I found

myself looking forward to getting killed, as then, at least, one
would be rid of this intolerable misery.[32]

Perhaps it was this proximity to madness that compelled Bion to regard
dream as a form of emotional achievement. Even a nightmare, he once
proposed, represents a kind of freedom compared to being caught and
confined to "the pale illumination of daylight."[33]

Once he entered psychoanalytic training after the war, Bion began to
treat dream-life as a particularly important state of mind. Like Freud, he
never tired of pointing out to his readers that just because this state of
mind changes—just because we happen to "wake up"—does not mean
that the significance of the sights, journeys, and "stray thoughts" that come
to us in dreams should be dismissed. Among his various essays, memoirs,
and lectures, Bion's concise book *Learning from Experience* elevates the significance of dreams by treating them as a central model of thinking, or
more specifically, as a central model of the *capacity* for thinking. Building
on Melanie Klein's description of unconscious fantasies as the structuring agents of the internal world, Bion proposed that dreaming provides a
key emotional function: dreams serve as an indispensable mental space or
"container" in which to process the emotional content of our experiences.
In this view, dreaming is something much more than a process for allaying
psychic tension in order to maintain sleep, as Freud initially imagined. Here
dream becomes the exemplary form of unconscious thinking about emotional experience, a heightened form of conversation with one's internal
objects. Interpretation is less significant in Bion's view; narrating one's
dreams is simply a kind of publishing of the symbolic work that has already
taken place. Moreover, for Bion, the dream's working-through of emotions and sense impressions does not differ significantly from the psychical processing occurring during waking life. He regarded nocturnal dreams
as exemplars that illustrate the larger activity of *dream-life,* a mode of functioning that is going on all the time, while we are asleep or awake.

Perhaps most significant for present purposes, Bion proposed that
dreams provide a "contact barrier" that both separates external reality from
the fantasies of the internal world *and* simultaneously generates a point
of safe passage between these two realms. In this respect, the analyst stayed
close to classical theory in which dreams carry the function of censorship
and resistance, which is to say, they help preserve "protective shield"
against elements, which, if allowed to penetrate into consciousness would

overwhelm and dominate the mind. In a rare example from *Learning from Experience*, Bion describes a man having a conversation with a friend. In the course of this everyday interaction, the man must convert the sense impressions and raw material of the conversation into emotionally digested thoughts. In Bion's terms this involves converting raw "beta-elements" into digested "alpha-elements." It is thanks to something like a dream— a membrane-like contact barrier—that the man can continue uninterrupt-edly to be "awake" to the fact that he is talking to his friend, but "asleep" to unknown truths, which would, if they could penetrate consciousness, flood his mind, disturbing his capacity for thought: "The dream," Bion writes, "makes a barrier against mental phenomena which might overwhelm the patient's awareness that he is talking to a friend, and, at the same time, makes it impossible for awareness that he is talking to a friend to over-whelm his phantasies."[34] Preserving the essential difference between inter-nal and external world phenomena, together with filtering the excitations arising from the latter, is perhaps the sine qua non of mental health. As Freud proposed in *Beyond the Pleasure Principle*, and as any number of war memoirs (including Bion's) corroborate, it is precisely this fundamental aspect of mental functioning that can break down during the successive shocks of modern warfare. It is a mistake to think the incendiaries of war only aim to breach the armor that shields human bodies. This violence also targets the fragile membranes that protect the mind.[35]

This conceptualization of dream as a "contact barrier" is elaborated in the work of French analyst Didier Anzieu. In his influential book *The Skin Ego*, Anzieu elaborates what he calls "the film of the dream." He uses the French term *pellicule* to designate two distinct functions of this psychical object: first, the dream works like the fine membranes or skin that protects and envelops certain parts of plant and animal organisms. In the second sense, Anzieu uses the term to refer to the film used in photography and cinema, the transparent strip of plastic that is coated with a light-sensitive emulsion to record the visual image. Like Bion, Anzieu regards the dream as a protective shield *and* as an impressionable surface, capable of register-ing mental images that are often visual in nature. Anzieu imagines these impressions can be strung together in an animated sequence, as we see in the cinema: "The film may be defective, the reel may get stuck or let light in, and the dream is erased. If everything goes well, we can on waking develop the film, view it, re-edit it or even project it in the form of a narrative told to another person."[36] Anzieu's metaphor also keeps close to classical dream theory, especially in the way Freud initially asked us to visualize the psychic apparatus as an optical instrument.

What is particularly significant about *The Skin Ego* is Anzieu's idea that the purpose of dream is to repair our psychic skin. Mending is required not only because of the dangers that the mind faces at night—the way the ego can come apart during sleep—but also from the encroachments one suffers during waking hours. This thesis adds strength to Kristeva's claim that the imaginary provides the primary shield for attacks on our being. In Anzieu's view, the fact that almost everyone dreams almost every night suggests that this particular mental object serves the vital function of daily reconstructing our psychic "envelope," filling in the narcissistic wounds that pierce the fragile ego on a regular basis. One can imagine the heightened need for this dream-film in times of social and political crisis such as the London Blitz. If anxiety works as a first defense—a defense by affect, protecting its subject against fright—then the dream-film provides a second kind of defense: a defense by representation. Whether produced by a serious trauma or by an accumulation of microtraumas, the holes in the ego are transposed by the work of representation to locations where the scenario of the dream can then unfold. In this process the holes can be sealed, filled in by the film of images: "The dream-film," Anzieu proposes, "represents an attempt to replace a deficient tactile envelope with a visual envelope, both finer and flimsier, but also more sensitive: the protective shield function is re-established *a minima*; the function of the inscription of traces and their transformation into signs is, by contrast, intensified."[37] In times of crisis, a fine and yet flimsy visual envelope is called to stand in as a protective shield for the mind.

Lee Miller's photographic work throughout the Blitz provides but one example of the way artistic works can provide a venue for this important symbolic elaboration, indeed, how such work effectively shields the populace from political violence. Among the most disturbing aspects of air war is surely the uncanny laws of blast. Bombs can render organized city space into a chaotic field of debris in a matter of seconds. They can, of course, do the same to bodies.[38] Simply moving through London's streets on any given morning during the Blitz likely meant coming into contact with an unusually intense array of sensations and raw sense impressions—"beta-elements" in Bion's terms—that required a significant amount of psychological processing in order for the city dweller to retain a sense of meaning of their environment, to hold a coherent sense of the world in mind. Some of Miller's less successful images, her "outtakes," attempt to register this destruction directly, in a kind of quasi-documentary style. But there is a distinct difference, Bion teaches us, between simply registering impressions and sensations and *learning from them*. It takes a great deal of symbolic labor to grapple with the chaos of this emotional experience, to transform incoherent debris into signs that can carry and hold meaning.

One of Miller's most arresting photographs of the Blitz depicts the shattered dome of the main building of University College. This site already carried considerable symbolic weight. Founded in 1826, University College was the first institution to be established on an entirely secular basis and the first to admit women on equal terms with men. Damage to these

Lee Miller, "Roof of University College," London, England, 1940. Copyright Lee Miller Archives, England, 2016. All rights reserved. www.leemiller.co.uk.

buildings, therefore, might have caught Miller's eye for more than one reason. Gauging from her contact sheets, at first the photographer attempted to capture the destruction directly.[39] As any one of us might do, she seems to have wandered into the atrium and angled her camera up toward the gaping hole in the dome. But this view does not capture the distinct emotional character of the Blitz; it fails to convey the field of destructive torrents, the unreal reality of living in a city that is being slowly, methodically destroyed by bombs that fall night after night.

Eventually Miller turned her attention away from the ceiling, letting her gaze wander downward toward the fragile human domain. She began to focus her favored Rolleiflex twin-lens camera on the ground. Rain seems to have poured through the shattered roof, leaving a pool of water on the stone floor below. Her final composition shows the shattered dome as a watery reflection, a surreal presentation that is unabashedly, indeed, compulsively beautiful.[40] One can see here how photography can lend itself to the imaginary, serving as an exemplary instrument to defend against air war's destruction of civilian life. Miller has managed to reinject a devastated landscape with all the salubriousness of dream-life. Her composition is built largely through negative space and yet this very negativity somehow endows the image with its potency. The picture manages to create a contemplative emotional space that is tinged with a palpable sense of loneliness, a feeling, which in turn, manages to open a sense of timeliness in which something lost might yet be recovered. The photograph both registers the terrible bomb damage and provides a delicate, visual shield against its destructive force. In short, Miller transfigures this material and psychological devastation into something sublime. Through such images spectators can catch a glimpse of all that air war seeks to destroy, and simultaneously, a means to preserve human life.

CHAPTER 5

The Colonial Defense

The Little Rotting Cat Dream

Can the subaltern (as woman) speak? . . . She writes with her body.
—Gayatri Chakravorty Spivak, *Can the Subaltern Speak?*

ON DECEMBER 6, 1961, the day of Frantz Fanon's death, French police seized copies of his newly published *Les damnés de la terre* from Paris bookshops. The book had been deemed seditious, in part, because of its incendiary call to arms. Fanon's opening chapter seemed declarative in this respect: "The colonized man liberates himself in and through violence."[1] At the time, the Algerian War of Independence—from the midst of which the thirty-six-year-old author was writing—had been raging for almost seven years. But the little book managed to reach well beyond this particular bloody anticolonial struggle to set fire to a whole generation.

When an English-language edition, *The Wretched of the Earth*, appeared a few years later, it went through five printings within the span of a year. As the story goes, the book had a decisive influence on Bobby Seale and Huey Newton's decision to found the Black Panther Party. The two had read it together in 1966 while they were still students at Merritt College. In the early 1970s, Steve Biko read aloud from it to the students and followers who gathered in his dorm room at the University of Natal in South Africa—the official meeting place and intellectual center of the Black Consciousness movement. And at some point during his initial imprisonment from 1973 to 1976, Bobby Sands, a young member of the Irish Republican Army, pulled *The Wretched of the Earth* down off the shelves of the library in the notorious HM Prison Maze—the same site where he would later die during a hunger strike in 1981. Fanon had talked of setting Africa ablaze, but by the late 1960s, his book had helped set more than one continent on fire.[2]

Perhaps today, more than a half century later, no one needs to be reminded that Fanon called for violence as a purifying antidote to the brutality of colonialism. This particular portrait of the young Martinican psychiatrist-turned-revolutionary has become something of an enduring caricature. Jean-Paul Sartre's infamously igneous preface to the book undoubtedly played a part. Discussions of *The Wretched of the Earth* often devote as much time to Sartre's contribution as they do to Fanon's text.

But not everyone was taken by the revolutionary spirit of the times: in the years immediately following his death, Fanon's work received more than its share of spurious attacks. Even Hannah Arendt couldn't help but join the growing chorus. In an essay that first appeared in the *New York Review of Books* in 1969, and which subsequently became the basis for her own book titled *On Violence,* Arendt anxiously tried to defuse some of Fanon's insurrectionary force—first by reminding readers of the larger "insanity" of the nuclear threat, and then by offering a series of (unasked for) lessons about the history of social change.[3] She admonished "the new preachers of violence" for being unaware of their "decisive disagreement" with Marxist teachings, complaining that they have inadvertently reversed the trajectory of revolutionary history: "The emergence of a new society was preceded, *but not caused,* by violent outbreaks, which [Marx] likened to the labor pangs that precede, but of course do not cause, the event of organic birth."[4] Arendt had a larger stake in this particular metaphor—she used *On Violence* to reassert her thesis that acting with a view to freedom is the human answer to the fundamental condition of natality—but in hindsight, her response to the liberation movements of the 1960s seems more than a little overwrought, itself a kind of caricature—in this case that of an aging academic scolding fiery youth for their ignorance of political history.

In the decades after this revolutionary period, Fanon has enjoyed a series of rebirths. In the 1980s and 1990s, theorists such as Homi Bhabha, Stuart Hall, Edward Said, and Françoise Vergès, among others, elaborated and extended various aspects of his restless thought, reinstating him as a key voice of decolonization and Third Worldism, but also of the contemporary postcolonial condition. Others continued to see his body of work as rife with contradiction. Fanon's Tunisian colleague, Albert Memmi, saw his political claims as, at best, specious statements born out of his particular tragedy, his "neurosis" as a split subject whose denial of his Martinican origins "poisoned his soul . . . as it has poisoned the soul of every young colonialized individual who has become conscious of his condition."[5] It may be that there are as many versions of Fanon as there are readers. As Henry Louis Gates Jr. summarily put it, Fanon "is a Rorschach blot with legs."[6]

Perhaps not surprisingly, my own attention falls on Fanon's use of dream-life. While some critics make much of the distinction between his early writings, which elaborate the particular schisms that the colonial situation generates in psychic life, and his later, more overtly revolutionary concerns, it bears pointing out that Fanon maintained an unwavering interest in dream-life.[7] Dreams play an important part in his first book, *Black Skin, White Masks,* and this alternative thought-landscape is equally significant to his last book, *The Wretched of the Earth.* While he undoubtedly became more invested in overturning the concrete material disparity caused by the colonial partitioning of the world, Fanon maintained a steady interest in this alternative thought-landscape. Indeed, he regularly seized upon dream-life as a key site in which individuals seek to negotiate—often under great duress—their freedom from colonial domination.

Part of Fanon's interest in dream-life can be explained by his professional training. The great majority of his career was spent in the clinic. He practiced psychiatry in France, in Algeria, and even in Tunisia during the years of his exile. In fact, he actively practiced—both in terms of writing clinical papers and treating patients—up until the last year of his life. This dimension of Fanon's work is often underestimated. Much like his political writings, his professional life was spent quarreling with the dominant discourse of his day—a quarrel that expressed itself, among other ways, in his particular style of working with dreams. Fanon's approach privileged the dreamer's social situation over timeless structures of psychical conflict. As he famously put it in the introduction to *Black Skin, White Masks,* he was not interested in "timeless truths."[8] Instead, Fanon emphasized the *sociogenic* factors—the geographic, historical, cultural, and social particularities of a community. For the psychiatrist, the "veritable apocalypse" of colonialism was the precipitating factor for the disturbances in his patients' mental life.[9] And as his extraordinary clinical notes show, dream-life became one of the most dramatic theatres in which Algeria's colonial war played out.

Part of the enduring significance of Fanon's work is his insistence on treating psychical life as integral to the larger project of political liberation. For the psychiatrist, the question of freedom had both a material *and* a psychological dimension. He regarded the structural transformation of society—and Algeria's independence from France, in particular—as indivisibly tied to the conflicts occurring at the level of the individual human personality. The penultimate chapter of *The Wretched of the Earth,*

"Colonial War and Mental Disorders," is decisive in this respect. Often overlooked, this chapter consists almost entirely of clinical notes—short vignettes concerning his Algerian and French patients, several of which include dream-reports. In this chapter, I read this clinical material as offering one of the most complex and ambivalent accounts of colonial violence that exists among Fanon's oeuvre. In this respect, I follow Alice Cherki's view that Fanon was a "thinker about violence, not its apologist."[10] In his case studies, Fanon displays some of his most intricate thinking about the ways violence works in the colonial theater. More specifically, these clinical notes show the ways colonial violence migrates through a principle of *displacement,* or what Freud might have referred to as *Verschiebung* (in German: movement, shift). Sometimes these displacements involve a shift of action, but more often the shift involves a substitute object. In both cases, Fanon's material offers important evidence of the unconscious dimensions of this political conflict.

There is a caveat. Vexingly, none of Fanon's published clinical notes include Algerian women's voices—even as this material provides a profusion of indirect evidence about the gross physical, sexual, and psychological abuse women suffered during the Algerian War.[11] It was widely known that French troops systematically used torture and rape to terrorize and shame the Algerian community, and Fanon would certainly have read Simone de Beauvoir's 1960 article in *Le Monde* about the sexual torture of the Algerian nationalist Djamila Boupacha, which "aroused the most extraordinary storm, not only in France but all over the world."[12] Traces of this form of violence are evident in Fanon's clinical notes, but he never acknowledged or analyzed this particular issue directly, despite his affirmed commitment to cataloging colonial brutality. In short, Fanon's definition of colonial violence does not seem to include sexual violence, and in his clinical work, women are all too often relegated to the role of speaking with their bodies.

There is no easy way to address this problem, at least not without the risk of transforming these subjects into objects by ventriloquizing on their behalf. In light of this ubiquitous dilemma in the historical record, Gayatri Spivak has suggested a method of "measuring silences": she asks readers to pay careful attention to what a work does *not* say.[13] Spivak is doubtful about whether subaltern women can be heard. Others have treated this thorny problem as a question of speaking *about* these historical silences without presuming to speak *for* them directly.[14] There are, in other words, significant impediments to thinking about the practice of freedom here, not least of which are the blind spots in Fanon's own body of thought. Wandering around the colonial outposts of dream-life will require equal parts caution and alchemy.

The Time Is Now

To oversimplify a complex body of work, Fanon promoted a two-step form of political education: awaken the mind to the realities of the world and reinvent the soul. The reinvention is necessary because the awakening is a rude one. His own devastating encounter with the effects of colonialism came early. In 1944, near the end of the Second World War, when Fanon was just eighteen years old, a Free French Forces ship landed in Martinique to invite all able-bodied young men to shed blood for their country. (Martinique was—and still is—an overseas region of France, which is to say, an official part of the Republic as opposed to a colony.) Full of idealism, Fanon joined the all-black battalion that eventually sailed to Casablanca for basic training. This was not his first experience with colonial racism, but the trip proved to be a decisive one. The Free French Forces camp at El Hajeb was a divided world akin to the Manichaean one that Fanon describes in *The Wretched of the Earth*: the West Indians were considered "semi-Europeans" and were billeted in separate barracks from their Arab and African counterparts. Fanon's battalion was given separate rations and they were issued standard French army uniforms while Arab troops wore *chechia*: fezzes, red flannel belts, and jerkins. Fanon's biographer, David Macey, reports that violent fights broke out over access to the brothels and a "Mobile Field Brothel" had to be brought in for the exclusive use of the Martinican contingent.[15]

After a short stop in Algeria, where Fanon was deeply affected by the sight of Arab children fighting savagely for the scraps of bread thrown to them by the troops (this scene makes a memorable appearance at the end of *The Wretched of the Earth*), his regiment was sent to France. By all accounts, he fought bravely until he was wounded in Colmar, but his division was nevertheless "whitened" when the press arrived to capture the scenes of the Allied march into Germany. Even the liberation festivities were tainted by racism: late in *Black Skin, White Masks*, Fanon offers a painful description of the way French women backed away, "faces filled with a fear that was not feigned," when black soldiers asked them to dance.[16] This can be read as the precursor to one of the most famous scenes of the book, when, several years later, on a cold day in Lyon, Fanon encountered a young French child who exclaimed: "Look a negro! . . . Mama, see the negro! I'm frightened!" First in Africa, and then in Europe, Fanon faced the crushing realization that in the eyes of much of the world he was not simply a French citizen as his Martinican upbringing had led him to believe, but rather "an object among other objects . . . a non-being . . . a *nègre*."[17]

In his early work, Fanon leaned upon the concepts and language of phenomenology to describe this awakening to the racist reality of colonialism. A person's sense of existence, he argued, is marked by their embodied, historical relationship to the world, by one's "lived experience" (*expérience vécue*). The phrase, borrowed from Maurice Merleau-Ponty, is one of the central terms in *Black Skin, White Masks*.[18] Merleau-Ponty argued that human agency is derived from our capacity to structure our body's relation to the world. The body is positioned as the locus of freedom to the extent that we have agency in the construction of a "corporeal schema," which in turn allows us to participate in the transformation of the social and cultural fabric. This sense of inhabiting a particular time and space is the basis for an embodied kind of communication with the world. As Merleau-Ponty famously claimed, "The body is our medium for having a world."[19] In contrast, Fanon went to pains to describe how, far from offering freedom, the white mythos of blackness seals the black body into a crushing state of objecthood, indeed, locks subjects in an alienated sense of unfreedom.

At home, in Martinique, Fanon might have had an intellectual awareness of the racialized dimensions of colonialism, but he had not yet fully faced the "lived experience" of the white imagination of blackness. His encounters in Europe and Africa provided the painful education. Once thus introduced to the world, he felt his prior sense of his body explode and he was forced to create a new, "historico-racial" corporeal schema: "The elements I used had been provided for me not by 'residual sensations and perceptions primarily of a tactile, vestibular, kinesthetic, and visual character,' but by the other, the white man, who has woven me out of a thousand details, anecdotes, stories."[20] The larger colonial situation means the black subject enters into the arena of intersubjective relations with a history that is already given. For this reason, Fanon argues, the colonized subject struggles to maintain his or her internally constituted bodily freedom under the white gaze. And once one has encountered this painful, corporeal sense of *being for others,* there can be no return to an internally derived body image. Even worse, the alienating white gaze can become internalized—or "epidermalized," as Fanon puts it—resulting in a dizzying sense of despair, nausea, and abjection.[21] Attempting to summarize the book's argument can only muffle its impact; *Black Skin, White Masks* is a graphic demonstration of the ways lived experience is an inescapably racialized affair.

Fanon's embodied sense of subjectivity infuses his entire corpus, including his approach to dream-life. The psychiatrist's first foray into dream interpretation comes in the fourth chapter of *Black Skin, White Masks*, where he discusses seven dreams from seven Malagasy individuals: "seven narratives that open the unconscious to us, and in six of them we find a dominant theme of terror. Six children and an adult tell us their dreams, and we see them trembling, seeking flight, unhappy."[22] These seven dreamers are not, however, Fanon's patients. As he reports, the dreams were initially reported in Octave Mannoni's 1950 study, *The Psychology of Colonization* (retitled *Prospero and Caliban* in the 1964 version), which Fanon describes as an "honest" but "dangerous" book. He devotes the entire fourth chapter of his own text to an extended critique of one of Mannoni's claims: that colonized peoples suffer from a "dependency complex."

Mannoni wrote his book in 1948 while he was stationed in Madagascar where he had first served as a philosophy teacher, and then, as the head of the colony's information service.[23] His long tenure as an administrator of the French colony is not insignificant: *The Psychology of Colonization* was written, in part, as a response to a rebellion that began in 1947 and that was met with what Maurice Bloch has called "one of the bloodiest episodes of colonial repression on the African continent."[24] After a frustrated attempt to achieve independence through political and legal channels, an anticolonial uprising led by the Mouvement Démocratique de la Rénovation Malgache began in March 1947. The initial revolts resulted in the death of 350 French soldiers and 200 civilians. The French responded by bringing 18,000 troops to the island nation, many of which had been rerouted from places in Africa, most notably Senegal. They used the occasion of the Madagascar revolt to perfect their new techniques of colonial warfare, what they euphemistically termed "pacification." Common tactics included torture, execution, the burning of villages, rape, and the mutilation of the dead. After a yearlong campaign in which the revolt was summarily repressed, the high commissioner reported to the French National Assembly that approximately 90,000–100,000 Malagasy had been killed.[25]

Despite Mannoni's position as a colonial agent during this period, *The Psychology of Colonization* does not directly discuss the Malagasy revolt or its bloody reprisal.[26] The study is a sweeping theoretical enterprise that attempts to explain and account for the psychology of colonization and racism in general, going so far as to sketch an evolutionary theory that the author argued was applicable to all individual psychological development and to the whole of humankind. It is against this sweeping universalism that Fanon aims his critique. When Mannoni argues, "The Malagasies' dreams faithfully reflect their overriding need for security and protection," Fanon coolly retorts, "one should not lose sight of the real."[27]

The thrust of Fanon's critique drew upon his particular sense of lived experience to add a grounded, embodied dimension to Mannoni's abstract theorizations. In the epilogue to the first section of *The Psychology of Colonialism*, Mannoni briefly acknowledges that the seven dreams were recorded at "a time of public disturbance," but he dismisses the significance of this situation because the dreamers "had seen nothing of the disorders."[28] Describing the Madagascar revolt as a "public disturbance" follows in the French tradition of referring to their colonial wars through euphemism. (It was not until 1999, for instance, that the French Assembly allowed the Algerian War to be publicly acknowledged as such.)

Mannoni notes that most of the dreams were collected in schools in the form of French homework, which suggests he was working with a collection of documents as opposed to engaging the children directly.[29] He offers no comment on this context and instead baldly presents each dream-report followed by an interpretation. Here is how he frames Razafi's dream:

> *Dream of a fourteen-year-old boy, Razafi.* He is being chased by (Senegalese) soldiers who "make a noise like galloping horses as they run," and "show their rifles in front of them." The dreamer escapes by becoming invisible; he climbs a stairway and finds the door of his home.
>
> The sexual significance of the rifle is obvious. The sound of the galloping horses and the desire to be invisible are probably explained by the fact that the child has witnessed the sexual act: he has both *heard* and *seen*.[30]

Mannoni interprets the children's dreams as if they had no history or context, as if these thought-landscapes contained an unchanging set of symbols and timeless truths, or worse, as if they furnished evidence of some innate deficiency in the Malagasy personality. A fourteen-year-old girl's dream about being chased and subsequently impaled by a fierce black ox provides proof of a "mutilation complex," which Mannoni claims is due to the island's circumcision rituals.

Fanon reproduces each of the seven dreams in his own book, but omits Mannoni's interpretation, effectively excising the colonizer's imposition of meaning. In fact, Fanon refrains from offering any interpretation of the dreams' meaning, but instead attempts to provide cultural context by way of a report from Madagascar's capital, which includes testimony about the torture being perpetuated on the local population by Senegalese policemen acting on behalf of the French. These enclosures are meant to add details about the social situation, to ground to the children's dreams in the milieu of their gestation—to expose the colonial violence that provides the backdrop for these nightmares:

> What must be done is to restore this dream to its *proper time,*
> and this time is the period during which eighty thousand natives
> were killed—that is to say, one of every fifty persons in the
> population; and to its *proper place,* and this place is an island of
> four million people, at the center of which no real relationship can
> be established, where dissension breaks out in every direction,
> where the only masters are lies and demagogy. One must concede
> that in some circumstances the *socius* is more important than the
> individual.[31]

Where Mannoni treats symbolism as something universal, Fanon insists on a concrete relation to the dreamer's material world: "The rifle of the Senegalese soldier is not a penis but a genuine rifle, model Lebel 1916."[32] The cloth of our dreamscapes is not made from an immutable storehouse of symbols, Fanon insists, but rather is woven from specific objects that the dreamer has perceptually seized from the material world.

Fanon's approach to dream-life not only reverses the predominant thinking of the time, but it also forecasts advances that would eventually arrive in psychoanalytic theory. By the late 1960s and 1970s, clinical theorists such as George Devereux and Hanna Segal began to break with the presiding view represented by Ernst Jones's 1916 "Theory of Symbolism." Where Jones insisted that "a given symbol has a constant meaning which is universal," analysts began to argue for the significance of *symbolic function-ing* (and the inhibition of this functioning). In this revised view, the mean-ing of a given symbol was often overdetermined and must be understood within the dreamer's lived cultural and historical context.[33] While the par-ticular mechanisms of the dream-work might remain constant, dream-life gradually came to be understood as highly idiosyncratic and inseparable from the individual's particular relationship to her environment. This dif-ference in approach yields a dramatically different mode and method of interpretation: where the children's dreams led Mannoni to posit a theory that colonial subjects suffer from a "dependency complex," Fanon viewed the dreams as evidence of a population under duress. The nightmares were attempts to process the cultural devastation surrounding them—irruptions of a traumatic reality into sleep.

File under: Displacement

Fanon's critical praxis intensified during his time in Algeria. In 1953, disillu-sioned by his experiences in Europe, the psychiatrist accepted an appoint-ment at Blida-Joinville Psychiatric Hospital, located in the city of Blida, about fifty kilometers southwest of Algiers. As one of Fanon's biographers describes, Blida had become Algeria's "capital of madness," largely because of the presence of the sprawling state institution that provided care for the mentally ill.[34] The Blida-Joinville Hospital opened in 1933, and by 1953, it was the largest psychiatric hospital in Algeria with some twenty-five hun-dred beds. Fanon was one of four *médécins-chefs*, each of whom had interns or housemen working under them. In a way, his life in Algeria was more comfortable than it had ever been before: Fanon was paid well, his family was provided with pleasant accommodations, and the hospital itself was modern and well equipped. But corruption was endemic: colonial doctors regularly swindled the local population (charging vast sums for injections of saline, for instance, claiming it was penicillin) and an overtly racist mind-set predominated. Psychiatric practice in the region was dominated by the so-called Algiers School, led by the French psychiatrist Antoine Porot. This approach attempted to justify the colonial mission in psychiatric terms, invoking biological theories of heredity to explain the "Arab syn-drome," for instance. When Fanon arrived in Algeria in 1953, doctors—like the magistrates, policemen, lawyers, and journalists—were expected to act as civilizing agents against the "rudimentary instincts" and "primitive mentality" of the local population.

It is this compromised professional world that the psychiatrist condemns in the next-to-last chapter of *The Wretched of the Earth,* "Colonial War and Mental Disorders." The clinical material gathered in this section of the book dates from 1954 to 1959, a period that overlaps with the Algerian War, during which time Fanon treated patients in Algeria (at Blida-Joinville Hospital and in private practice), and then, after he went into exile in Tunisia, at the National Liberation Front's (FLN) medical facilities. The chapter is among the least studied portions of Fanon's oeuvre, perhaps because, as the author himself remarked, "these notes on psychiatry will be found ill-timed and singularly out of place in such a book."[35] In my reading, however, these clinical vignettes offer one of the most compelling albeit enigmatic portraits of colonial violence that Fanon provided.[36]

The chapter is organized into four lettered sections, each of which contains several cases. Although he claims that his approach is not scientific, and that he has avoided "semiological, nosological, or therapeutic discussion," he does concede some technical qualifications, calling the cases typical "psychotic reactions." Fanon nevertheless gives priority to the situation that triggered the reaction, and while some of the cases have more specific causes than others, Fanon states that, in his opinion, the principal triggering factor is "the bloody, pitiless atmosphere, the generalization of inhumane practices, of people's lasting impression that they are witnessing a veritable apocalypse ... which very often takes the aspect of a genuine genocide, this war, which radically disrupts and shatters the world."[37] The cases themselves display a startlingly wide range of ways that the war's shattering force manifested at the individual level—both in combatants and civilians: hallucinations (including paranoia and somatic delusions), behavioral and emotional disorders (violent outbursts, sadistic tendencies, sleepwalking), severe anxiety and depressive disorders (phobias, anorexia, sleeplessness), and a suite of psychosomatic illnesses.

Fanon's main argument is that these symptoms are evidence for the ways that colonial violence profoundly "dislocates" the personality of its subjects.[38] The claim can be understood as a variation of the more familiar concept of displacement. The idea is that the psychical intensity associated with a particular thought or idea can become detached and run along associative pathways, that the affective or emotional force of particular experience can "slip" from one location to another.[39] Freud describes displacement as one of the four mechanisms of dream-work, one of the common ways in which meaning can be shifted: by transferring value from one site to another so as to find a solution to a conflict.[40] He characteristically borrowed and adapted one of Nietzsche's phrases to describe displacement as "a transvaluation of psychical values."[41] Significantly, Freud also observed displacement to be at work in various neurotic and psychotic illnesses and the modes of defense employed in each—perhaps most famously in his case study of Little Hans, the boy who suffered from a phobia of horses. In *The Analysis of Defense*, Anna Freud continued these clinical observations, elaborating the defense mechanisms that grow out of primary process functioning.[42]

Fanon's case studies seem to suggest a special intimacy between colonialism and the mechanism of displacement. In a sense, the entire colonial project can be understood as a large-scale transvaluation—an attempt to transfer the laws, language, and culture of one nation-state to another territory. Psychoanalysis itself became a colonial *dispositif* in service of this project, as Fanon's critique of Mannoni's work suggests. But as Fanon shows, the psychotic outbreaks that his patients display represent both a symptom but also an attempt at self-cure, an unconscious effort to "outwit the conflict using the wrong, but nevertheless economic channels."[43] While all of his cases bear evidence of the devastating and enduring effects of this war, a small handful offer especially vivid accounts of the ways that violence can be displaced, how unresolved conflicts can be carried from one situation to another through the use of a substitute. Collectively they provide a portrait of the colonial landscape as dramatically out of joint:

> *Case no. 3 of Series A concerns D——, a nineteen-year-old former student and soldier in the National Liberation Army (the armed wing of the FLN). The patient had attempted suicide twice before seeing Dr. Fanon, and suffered from pernicious insomnia and blocking (when a gesture or phrase is begun and then interrupted without apparent reason). D—— also suffered from hallucinations, the most alarming of which was his sense of being "sucked by a vampire"—that his blood was being drained from his body by a woman who visited him at night. Fanon suspected this was a maternal image: D——revealed that his mother was killed at point-blank range by a French soldier and two of*

his sisters were taken into their barracks and never heard from again. Being the only man in the family, D—— reports that his sole ambition had always been to make life easier for his mother and sisters. After the loss of his family, he left school and joined the army. One day during a patrol, he visited to a large colonial estate where the manager was alleged to have killed two Algerian civilians. Only the manager's wife was at home, and the patrol decided to wait to see if the husband would return. While they waited, D—— kept looking at the wife, thinking of his mother. The woman grew more and more hysterical and threw herself on him, screaming and begging for mercy:

"The next minute she was dead. I'd killed her with my knife. My commander disarmed me and gave me orders to leave. I was interrogated by the district commander a few days later. I thought I was going to be shot, but I didn't give a damn. After that I began to vomit after eating and I slept badly. After that this woman would come every night asking for my blood. And what about my mother's blood?"

When D—— goes to bed, his room is invaded by a host of women, all duplicates of the woman he killed, all with gaping holes in their stomachs, all demanding their blood back. His room fills with a thundering waterfall of blood—his blood—which slowly revives and heals the women. Fanon reports that although these hallucinatory nightmares were lessened through treatment, D——'s personality remained seriously disorganized. Whenever he thinks of his mother, the disemboweled woman looms up. Fanon concludes: "As unscientific as it may seem, we believe only time will heal the dislocated personality of this young man."[44]

Series B includes an account of two Algerian boys aged thirteen and fourteen who were brought to Blida-Joinville hospital for a forensic examination, presumably with a view to establishing their degree of criminal responsibility in a murder case. The two boys had killed one of their friends, a European boy their own age, who they played with every Thursday afternoon on a hill behind their village. On one of these afternoons, the two boys held the victim down and stabbed him with a knife. Fanon asked why they done this to their friend. They insisted they were not angry with him, but on the contrary, that he was their best friend. They readily admitted that he had done nothing wrong, and yet:

"One day we decided to kill him because the Europeans want to kill all the Arabs. We can't kill the 'grown-ups', but we can kill someone like him because he's our own age." The elder of the two boys mentions that two of his family members were killed by the French in Rivet, a village outside Algiers. (Fanon explains in a footnote that in this infamous incident, the French militia dragged forty men from their beds one night and executed them on the spot.) When the psychiatrist presses the older boy, telling him that these things concern grown-ups, the boy responds: "But they kill children too." Fanon replies: "But that's no reason for killing your friend." The case report ends with the boy's chillingly depersonalized reply: "Well, I killed him. Now you can do what you like. . . . That's all there is to it."[45]

Case No. 5 in Series A involves R——, a thirty-year-old European police inspector who referred himself to Fanon because he was worried about his growing propensity for violence. R—— had begun smoking three packs of cigarettes a day, lost his appetite, and his sleep was disturbed by nightmares (showing "no particular distinguishing features"). His chief complaint is inexplicable bouts of violence: he had begun assaulting his children, including his twenty-month-old baby. When his wife tried to intervene, R——reports that he turned on her, beat her, and tied her to a chair, shouting: "I'm going to teach you once and for all who's the boss around here." The children began to scream and R—— eventually came to his senses. The next morning he decided to consult a "nerve specialist." He believed that his present problems stem from "the troubles":

"The fact is," he said, "we're now being used as foot soldiers. Those guys in government say there's not war in Algeria and the police force must restore law and order, but there *is* a war in Algeria. . . . The thing that gets me the most is the torture. Does that mean anything to you? . . . Sometimes I torture for ten hours. . . . It wears you out, of course. . . . Our problem is, are we able to get the guy to talk? It's a matter of personal success; we're sort of competing. We eventually messed up our fists. So we brought in the 'Senegalese.' But either they hit too hard and mess up the guy in thirty minutes, or not enough and nothing happens. In fact, you need to use your head for this kind of work. You need to know when to tighten your grip and when to loosen it. You have to have a feel for it. When the guy is ripe, there's no point in continuing to hit him."

R—— did not want to leave the police force. He knew his problems stemmed from the type of work he was being asked to do in the interrogation rooms, but he blamed "the troubles" and only wanted to be "straightened out" about the business with his wife at home. He asked Fanon, in plain, straightforward language, to help him torture Algerian patriots "without having a guilty conscience, without any behavioral problems, and with a total peace of mind."[46]

In each of these cases, the incidents of violence that marked a subject's life found a new venue of expression. One victim was substituted for another, although these occurrences could hardly be filed away as examples of so-called displaced aggression. Each case shows the way violence occurring in the colonial theater was compulsively repeated: a son murders a mother; children stab their friend; a husband tortures his family. What is repeated, moreover, is not simply the particular act, but also a larger structural alignment. In the first two cases, subjects who were initially passive (their kin were murdered at the hands of the French) became active agents, murderers in their own right. In the latter case, the torture continues in a new venue—the police inspector can no longer distinguish "work" from home, FLN suspect from family member. However different in their particulars, what each of the cases displays is the power of the mechanism of displacement: the way meaning can come unmoored from one place and lodged in another. Each example, moreover, puts pressure on the idea of intentionality: the repetition of the act of violence occurs seemingly without the agent's conscious consent, or in the children's case, under an emotional fog, as if they were sleepwalking. In the context of war, it seems primary process—the logic of the unconscious—vies for sovereign control.

Variations on the Right to Remain Silent

Perhaps the most complex and delicate example of displacement appears in Case No. 1 from Series A, which Fanon labeled *"Impotence in an Algerian following the rape of his wife."* This case concerns a twenty-six-year-old man, B——, who was referred through the medical services of the National Liberation Front. As with all his Algerian patients who did not speak French, Fanon treated the young man through an interpreter, a fact that has not gone unnoticed.[47] B—— displayed symptoms of persistent migraines and insomnia. In the first consultation, Fanon reports that he appeared lively, "a little too lively perhaps," because by the second day, B——'s smoke screen of optimism vanished and in his place was "a bedridden anorexic suffering from melancholic depression." It took several days for Fanon and his interpreter to reconstruct a coherent case history:

> *Before the war, B—— had worked as a taxi driver, and after joining the FLN, he transported leaflets, and eventually, commandos who were on route to various sites of attack. After a surprise raid, B—— was forced to abandon his taxi and go into hiding underground. He did not have an opportunity to visit or even alert his family of what had transpired. B—— was married and the couple had a twenty-month-old daughter. He went without news of his family for several months and was eventually sent abroad by the FLN. During this time, B—— attempted to have a sexual affair, but found he was impotent. Thinking his sexual failing might be due to fatigue from his ordeal, he tried again a few weeks later. The second attempt also failed. Upon advice from a comrade, he tried vitamin B12: a new attempt, a fresh failure. B—— disclosed to Dr. Fanon that a few moments before embarking on the sexual act, he had an irresistible urge to tear up a photo of his daughter. Fanon speculates that this symbolic connection could raise the possibility of an unconscious incestuous link between the liaison and B——'s daughter. But the conversation leads in another direction: B—— discloses a dream in which he witnesses the rapid rotting of a little cat that gives off a nauseating smell. The associations to this image are as follows: "This girl," B—— tells Fanon one day, referring to his daughter, "has something rotten inside her."[48] From this moment on, the patient's insomnia worsened, and despite a large dose of neuroleptics, he began expressing an alarming state of nervous anxiety.*
>
> *B—— then spoke for the first time of his wife. He laughingly declared, "She's tasted the French." There is some difficulty constructing the rest of the story. Apparently, after the raid that initially sent B—— into hiding, a long period passed when he had no contact with his family. Eventually he received a message from his wife asking him to forget her: "She had brought shame upon herself. He must no longer think of coming back to live with her." Alarmed at this cryptic message,*

B—— requested leave to make a secret trip home. The request was denied but steps were taken for a member of the FLN to contact B——'s wife and parents. Two weeks later a more detailed report arrived.

The report relayed a series of events beginning with the police arriving at B——'s home soon after his abandoned taxi had been discovered (with two machine gun magazines inside). Finding him absent, they detained his wife. She was interrogated and "slapped fairly violently for two days." On the third day a French soldier ordered the others out of the room and then raped her. Shortly afterward, a second soldier raped her in the presence of the others, telling her: "If you ever see that bastard your husband again, don't forget to tell him what we did to you." She was detained another week before being released. After the initial shock of this news, B—— threw himself into the cause. He traveled, collecting testimony from Algerian women who had been tortured and raped by the French, and at the same time, pushed his own personal misfortune to the background. He described being puzzled by the peasants who heroically volunteered to marry the young girls who had been made pregnant by their rapists. When pressed, B—— admitted that after the shock he only felt relief that his wife wasn't killed. He imagined that what happened would somehow free them to start over. He admitted that his marriage was a passionless arrangement, that he had been in love with his cousin, and that he accepted his wife only after his cousin was betrothed to another man. He had never grown very attached to his wife and, apart from mealtimes, they barely interacted.

B—— describes how it took him several weeks to realize that the French soldiers raped his wife "because they had been looking for me," that, in fact, she had been raped as punishment for keeping quiet:

"It was not a simple rape for want of anything better to do or out of sadism, as I had often seen in the *douars* [villages]; it was the rape of a tenacious woman who was prepared to accept anything rather than give up her husband. And that husband *was* me. That woman had saved my life and protected the network. It was my fault she had been dishonored. . . . I've made up my mind to take her back, but I still don't know how I'll react when I see her. And when I look at the picture of my daughter I often think she was dishonored as well. As if everything that had to do with my wife was rotten. If they had tortured her, if they had broken all her teeth or an arm, I wouldn't have minded so much. But that thing, how can you ever get over it? *And did she have to tell me about it?*"[49]

B—— *queries Fanon whether his "sexual failing" might be caused by his worrying. Fanon responds, "It's quite likely." An exchange ensues in which B—— asks the psychiatrist what he would do if their positions were reversed, whether he would take his wife back. Dr. Fanon responds affirmatively. It is not clear why, but after this session, B—— was able to tolerate talk of the political situation and his insomnia and anorexia lessened considerably. Within a few weeks he had rejoined his unit, confiding in Fanon that he had made a decision. Upon independence, he would return to his wife: "If it doesn't work out, I'll come and see you in Algiers."*

The case carries all of the complex turns of an ancient Greek tragedy, albeit one that is set in the Maghreb circa 1957: A war of independence has broken out, separating the protagonists of a loveless marriage. The husband goes off to fight the tyrant's forces on a distant front, during which time he meets a young woman and attempts to embark on a sexual affair. Meanwhile, at home, his rebelliousness is met with a brutal reprisal: his wife is raped by the tyrant's forces. This particular scene occurs offstage, so to speak. The information is delivered in the form of a letter, which eventually finds the husband while he is abroad. Even from afar, the contents of the tyrant's enigmatic message—initially written across his wife's body before being translated into speech—manage to work their torturous intent: the husband goes mad with guilt.

In this setting, Fanon would be cast in the role of the chorus, providing just enough background so the audience can follow the action, but also occasionally interacting with the characters, providing insight, and demonstrating the way we ought to respond to each turn in the plot. Perhaps a psychiatrist is the proper heir to this dramatic corpus. The concluding scene is decidedly ambiguous, indeed, almost modern in its unresolved tension: Fanon reports that the husband has recovered enough from his madness to return to war, and he makes plans to reunite with his wife upon its conclusion. But the audience is left questioning whether this reunion will ever transpire. The resolution—of the war, of the marriage, indeed, of the entire world this narrative has called into existence—is left painfully uncertain.

There are two peaks in this tragedy, at least in my imaginary restaging of it. One, of course, is the protagonist's dream. Perhaps this would best be staged as a vision: One night while interned in the asylum, B—— awakens to the sound of a small creature moving around in his room. He rises to see a little cat scuffling around in the corner. When he approaches the tiny creature, it rapidly putrefies before his eyes, emitting an evil smell. He begins to gag uncontrollably, backing away from the wretched thing and eventually succumbing to a violent fit of anxiety.

The creature's uncanniness is paramount, a signal that this dream-figure is already a substitute—an ersatz form of the young daughter. The dream can be understood in this sense as both symptom and cure: by shifting the rot to the daughter, by making this *little pussy* the site of noxious spoilage, the husband has discovered an ingenious way to return to his wife. Through the action of displacement, the wife is cleansed of the tyrant's violent assault, and therefore the husband can be cleansed of his guilt. The transformation offers an elegant solution to the abjection that permeates the case: its promises to allow both protagonists to recover a dimension of their dignity. But in this instance, the designs of the dream-work work more like an evacuation of indigestible material. While the conflicts of one generation might seem to be resolved by the displacement, the fate of the next is put into question. What will become of this little girl who has been coated—infected—with the filth of a war that precedes her? An Antigone in waiting, her future both uncertain and already decided.

Perhaps we could consider B——'s dream of the little rotting cat (and, indeed, many of the dreams in Fanon's clinical notes) as an example of what Michael Eigan names "damaged dream-work."[50] This is an instance when the processes of dream-work are themselves damaged by the damage they are trying to work with. Dreams attempt to limit and contain pain and generate new possibilities, but as Eigan shows, this function can be damaged and even blown away by the catastrophic trauma it tries to dispel and transform. Our most intimate psychic defense can itself break apart. On one level, this can mean that a thought fails to be incorporated into the larger network of thinking. For thoughts to be meaningful they have to be worked with, linked with other thoughts, lived and responded to. In psychosis, this linking functioning is severely damaged or destroyed. Damaged dreams are attempts to split off and jettison something that is felt to be unreal, something that cannot be emotionally metabolized or incorporated into the dreamer's psychical life.

Along this vein, we might also have to write in a scene for Madame B——, since the historical record fails to provide it. The case would seem to proffer proof for Gayatri Spivak's lament that the subaltern woman cannot be heard. As Spivak points out, not being heard is not quite the same thing as not speaking. Indeed, in one sense, the whole of this case turns on the wife's speech: it is her missive that occasions her husband's breakdown. The wretched query at the end of his dialogue reveals the origins of his torment: *Did she have to tell me about it?* To be fair, Madame B—— did decline to tell him at first, although perhaps it was the enigmatic nature of her initial message that drove him to pursue the rest of the story: *She had brought shame upon herself. He must not think of coming back to live with her.* Spivak might insist that pronouns are significant here: the "I" is denied to Madame B——. She falls conspicuously outside the mode of production of this narrative between Fanon and his patient, marking what the postcolonial theorist calls the "points of fadeout" in the writing of history, footprints that efface even as they disclose.[51] For Spivak, such female figures impose the largest demand on our techniques of retrieval and they cannot be taken in a rationalist mode: "they are the figures of justice as the experience of the impossible."[52]

Part of this impossibility turns on the problems of translation. Case no. 1 abounds in translation failure—or more to Spivak's point, it abounds in instances of translations that also efface. Not only did Fanon require a translator to mediate between himself and his patients, but the subsequent translators of Fanon's text have also left their mark. In the original French version, B—— is reported to say of his wife, *"Elle a goûté du Français."* This is, of course, already a translation of the man's original statement, which would probably have been uttered in Kabyle or Arabic. In the first English edition of Fanon's text, Constance Farrington offers this translation: "She's tasted the French." In the 2004 edition, Richard Philcox opts for a more euphemistic version: "She got a bit of French meat."[53]

But these multiple, fractious statements are already a translation of Madame B——'s own account of what happened to her. Indeed, the two separate letters mentioned in the case can be understood as two different translations of the rapists' message, which initially used Madame B——'s body as its medium: *If you ever see that bastard your husband again, don't forget to tell him what we did to you.* There is an important distinction to be made here between torture and rape, insofar as torture is designed to manipulate the tortured subject's relationship to speech, to produce a certain

kind of truth in the form of a confession, the status of which is performative.[54] If we believe that Madame B—— did indeed protect her husband and
his network, then the torture failed to produce this confessional speech.
The rape marks a shift in political strategy. Here the aim is to disturb the
social structure by violating the integrity of the desiring body. Rape inter-
venes upon the subject's speech indirectly; it uses the medium of the body
to conduct its communications, a bit like the apparatus from Kafka's story
about the penal colony—that dreadful machine that uses a needle-like
harrow to inscribe the sentence directly onto the body of the condemned, a
sentence the condemned is not told but rather *experiences* right on her body.
How could Madame B—— pass this dreadful script on to her husband?

The case begs for an entirely new account of Fanon's sense of "lived
experience," of the way in which sexual difference, like race, is *epidermalized* by colonial imperialism. While Spivak rightly cautions us against any
straightforward attempts to recover Madame B——'s speech, there is surely
much to be said about the forces that obscure our reading of such deep
silences in the historical record.

Intimate Revolt

There is something maddeningly attractive about the untranslatable—
those instances when something "goes silent in transit."[55] My attempt to animate the silences in Fanon's case studies is not designed to offer a definitive
reading so much as to underscore the psychiatrist's own warnings about
the cultural politics of interpretation. Dreams are psychic events derived
from a vast storehouse of lived experiences; imposing meaning from outside the cultural milieu can all-too-easily repeat the colonial gesture.

Fanon's cases also provide crucial evidence for the ways in which revolt
does not belong only to the manifest arenas of political action; freedom is
something that must be fought for and won in the life of the mind. While
political revolt has been the subject of concentrated analysis for several
centuries—in the modern sense at least since the time of the American
Revolution—this *internal* dimension of revolt, what Julia Kristeva calls
"intimate revolt," has received considerably less scrutiny.[56] For Kristeva,
overt political contestation is but one aspect of a much deeper mode of
human questioning and transformation. Dream-life represents one of the
chief points of access to this micro-political level. The dream-work's transformations provide a confrontation with the very unity of the law, being,

and the self. Because this process involves a fundamental transformation of the subject's relationship to meaning, our intimate revolts are intrinsically linked to public life and consequently have profoundly political implications. As Mr. B——'s dream avows, it is the most intimate battles that can provide the greatest hope for the reconstitution of the speaking being—the *little things* are key in our struggles for freedom.

· CHAPTER 6 ·

On Folding Force

WHEN ADOLF HITLER was named chancellor of Germany on
January 30, 1933, the Nazi Party led torchlight parades throughout
Berlin. This was neither the first nor the last time the Nazis employed such
spectacles, but the date could be said to mark the beginning of the party's
concerted attempt to lay claim to the night.

It was at this point that the nightmares began. Shortly after the Nazi
Party took power, Charlotte Beradt, a young Berlin-based journalist began
to awaken night after night bathed in perspiration, teeth clenched in terror.
On one of these nights, after dreaming of being hunted "from pillar to
post" by storm troopers, a new thought arrived: what if she wasn't the
only one?[1] What if the things that appeared in her nightmares were also
being visited upon other people? This startling thought set in motion the
seeds of a research project. Beradt quietly began to query people about
their dream-life.

Her suspicions were quickly confirmed. Herr S, a sixty-year-old manufacturer described as an "upright and self-confident" individual, revealed
that he had begun having a recurring nightmare three days after Hitler
seized power.[2] Beradt describes the dream as an exemplar of the "sheer
psychological torture" the Nazis perpetrated upon the citizenry, a parable
par excellence of how the totalitarian regime produced submissive subjects. Here is the manufacturer's dream:

> Goebbels [the Nazi minister for propaganda] was visiting my
> factory. He had all the workers line up in two rows facing each
> other. I had to stand in the middle and raise my arm in the Nazi
> salute. It took me half an hour to get my arm up, inch by inch.
> Goebbels showed neither approval nor disapproval as he watched
> my struggle, as if it were a play. When I finally managed to get my

arm up, he said just five words—"I don't want your salute"—then turned and went to the door. There I stood in my own factory, arm raised, pilloried right in the midst of my own people. I was only able to keep from collapsing by staring at his clubfoot as he limped out. And so I stood until I woke up.[3]

The nightmare never failed to produce a sense of humiliation in Herr S. His factory, where he had employed many an old fellow Social Democrat for more than twenty years, meant everything to him. Beradt reports that the manufacturer's nightmare recurred again and again in the dark days that followed, often incorporating new, mortifying details. Herr S seems to have been particularly sensitive to the Nazis' perverse pleasure in public humiliation. In one version, sweat poured down his face like tears, "as if I were crying in front of Goebbels." In another, he desperately searched his workers' faces for signs of sympathy only to be met with expressions of absolute emptiness. On one occasion the nightmare's symbolism was devastatingly, indeed, almost vulgarly clear. In this instance the violent struggle to lift his arm breaks the dreamer's spine—*brach ihm das Rueckgrat*.[4] The connotation is the same in German as in English: Herr S lacked the backbone to stand up to Hitler's minister for propaganda.

After hearing several such testimonies, Beradt began to believe that dream-life itself had come to be dictated by the dictatorship. She regarded the manufacturer's nightmare as indicative of the general atmosphere of coercion. Herr S's dream, she argues, was generated in the "very same workshop where the totalitarian regime constructed the mechanism that made it function."[5] And so her fleeting thought became a concerted plan: the journalist set out to document the dreams the regime had, so to speak, manufactured.

This turned out to be no easy task. People were reluctant and sometimes afraid to confide their dreams. Beradt reports a half a dozen instances in which individuals dreamed that it was forbidden to dream (but did so anyway). She canvassed a broad cross section of the population: students, secretaries, housewives, and lawyers. She did not reveal her purpose when she approached people, for she wanted "to avoid replies that were colored."[6] She also enlisted friends to help gather material, including a doctor who had a large practice and was able to query his patients unobtrusively. Altogether, she obtained material from more than three hundred people—a large sample by any standards—although she openly admits the limitations of her study: she failed to collect dream-reports from enthusiasts of the regime. Such individuals were not readily accessible to her: Beradt was the daughter of Jewish merchants.

When she was compelled to leave Germany in 1939, the journalist and her husband managed to find their way to New York, where she joined a community of exiles—a "tribe" of ex-Berliners that included Hannah Arendt and Heinrich Blücher. During the war, a New York–based leftist magazine called *Free World* published a short article about her collection of dreams. It was not until 1966, with Arendt's help, that she was able to publish a book-length study under the title, *Das Dritte Reich des Traums*. An English-language edition—*The Third Reich of Dreams*—quickly followed in 1968.

Some eighty years after she gathered them, Beradt's collection of dream-reports still has the power to startle. Their coiled potency is due, in part, to their distinctive mode of testimony. Dreams invariably fail to offer a documentary presentation of reality, and yet they are not consciously fabricated either. In this respect, these productions possess the status of neither fact nor fiction, but as the German historian Reinhart Koselleck points out, this does not prevent them from "belonging to life's reality." For Koselleck, the dreams Beradt collected represent an indispensable historical resource precisely because they testify to an "irresistible facticity of the fictive."[7] That is to say, it is precisely through their strange, seemingly fictional guise that dreams manage to offer a veritable index of the dreamer's lived experience.

Beradt was not the first person to suggest that our dream-landscapes are dramatically shaped by social and political forces, but her project represents one of the more systematic attempts to study this dynamic. The journalist did not seek out people's dream-life with a therapeutic intention in mind. Although she borrowed liberally from psychoanalytic ideas, her study draws rather different conclusions about the sources and significance of this terrain. Her claim that dream-life was "dictated by the dictatorship" lies some distance from Sigmund Freud's signal thesis, even as she furnishes evidence for his idea that dreams represent the fulfillment of an unconscious wish.[8] The journalist's position deviates most dramatically from the classical psychoanalytic view in the degree of power Beradt suggests the Nazis' possessed over interior life. In her mind, the dictatorship effectively colonized the unconscious of its citizens, implanting images and even whole plots in the minds of the populace.

Beradt's proposition is understandable. After the Reichstag Fire Decree of 1933, many of the key civil liberties of German citizens were nullified, and what once might have belonged to the private sphere had become grist for Nazi scrutiny. The journalist felt that her collection of dreams offered unique evidence for just how deeply "fear reaches down into the subconscious," revealing a hitherto unrealized connection between the individual and the political environment.[9] As one of her dreamers put it, fascism had created a "world without walls," and in such a world, nothing was safe— not even dream-life.[10]

Diaries of the Night

Had he lived to study Beradt's collection, I suspect Freud would have proposed a slightly more encouraging view. While the psychoanalyst was acutely aware that the furniture of dream-life is borrowed from the material world, and that the whole process of dream-formation is highly susceptible to suggestion and subject to censorship (the German noun *Zensur* appears prominently in *The Interpretation of Dreams*), he nevertheless believed that there was a fundamental part of the psyche that remained unassailable. Fear could certainly lend its power to the restricting, inhibiting force of the dream censor, but it could not radically modify the operations of the unconscious. Freud agreed that dreams are designed independently of the dreamers' conscious will, but he would almost certainly question Beradt's decision to credit the Nazis for authoring these "diaries of the night."[11] In contrast, I suspect Freud would have regarded the collection as offering evidence of the human being's radical freedom to assign meaning to experience. The activity of dreaming represents one of our primal means to exercise this fundamental freedom of thought. In dark times in particular, this activity provides one of our most formidable means to bend and transfigure the force of a disturbing reality.

The stakes of this interpretation rest on the way we define the human subject, or more specifically, on how we delineate the psychology of political subjugation. After the war, several waves of debate engaged this question by investigating the various processes of mass psychology (or "brainwashing," to use a popular term coined in the 1950s). These investigations made important inroads into the question of psychic manipulation as well as the significance of collectively working through past political violence. Theodor Adorno, for one, offered an important intervention in these debates in

1960, arguing on German State radio that National Socialism was alive and well in the unconscious life of citizens in the fledgling postwar democracy.[12]

As compelling as these subsequent studies are, Beradt's project poses a rather different entrée into the question of how the human psyche comes to be constituted and constrained by dark times. In contrast to investigating the operations of mass psychology, these individual dream-reports offer a more intimate kind of evidence about the effects of an oppressive political environment—they point toward a *micro*-economy of power relations. Evidently, a dream is not akin to the more obvious political gestures such as voting or marching in a parade, but this mental activity can still be understood as an important species of political thought. Indeed, Beradt's collection provides a prism through which to reconsider the ways political power—far from being simply impressed upon the psyche—represents a force each individual negotiates on a nightly basis. In turn, this particular *form* of thought might offer a new site to consider the psychological roots of resistance.

As the Nazi organizational leader Robert Ley once snidely proposed, "The only person in Germany who still leads a private life is the person who sleeps."[13] As vicious as this observation may be, it perhaps hits close to the mark. Dream-life can serve as one of our last and most important preserves to stage a claim for the freedom of thought—*in dream-life if nowhere else.*[14]

The Intransigence of Freedom

In a long article titled "The Subject and Power," Michel Foucault, like many before him, proposed that the emergence of fascism in the middle of the twentieth century was not something new, but rather only made the long-standing relationship between rationalization and the excesses of political power readily transparent. There was no need to wait for "bureaucracy or concentration camps to recognize the existence of such relations," he quipped.[15] In spite of its unique internal madness, Foucault insisted that fascism relied, in large part, on all-too-familiar forms of political rationality. The real question, as the philosopher saw it, is what to do with such an evident fact.

Like many of the Frankfurt School thinkers before him, Foucault rejected the idea of returning to reason. As he dryly remarked, "Nothing would be more sterile." Instead, he proposed a different strategy, another avenue toward a new economy of power relations. Rather than analyze power from the point of view of its internal rationality, the philosopher proposed to take the different forms of resistance as a starting point. His essay provides a blueprint for this new program of study (a project he would not live to complete) that consisted of examining the various modes and forms of resistance to the exercise of power as it applies in immediate, everyday life: the way children resist their parents' attempts to administer their lives, the way the mentally ill disassociate from dominant forms of psychiatry, or the quotidian strategies women utilize to resist patriarchy.

Foucault's proposed project relies on an important distinction between violence and power. While violence acts directly upon the body—either yoking or destroying the other—Foucault defined power as fundamentally relational. The exercise of power depends on maintaining the other as a subject who is capable of action—however unequally positioned. The philosopher does not downplay the profound effects institutions have in the establishment of these relationships. Throughout his career, Foucault devoted himself to elaborate analyses of the dividing practices by which institutions seek to categorize certain human beings as insane, diseased, or criminal. But as he came to realize, these institutional forces do not simply negate the subject's capacity for resistance. Indeed, as he provocatively described, "freedom must exist for power to be exerted.... The power relationship and freedom's refusal to submit cannot be separated."[16]

At the beginning of his last book, *The Care of the Self,* Foucault turned to the ancient practice of dream interpretation as a key site for analyzing these more intimate dimensions of power relations. As he outlines in detail, in the ancient world, dream interpretation served as an important method for an individual to engage in the formal practice of *epimelesthai sautou,* or "care of the self." Such practices provided a primary means by which individual freedom—and even civic liberty, to a degree—were achieved. For the Greeks, these formal execises were considered requirements in the pursuit of proper ethical conduct. To take care of the self was to equip oneself with certain truths about oneself: how could one govern others if one could not govern oneself? Self-examination was considered a necessary exercise in this respect, a formal practice of reflection that animated the internal world by doubling or *folding* aspects of the external world. Among the Greeks, dreaming and dream interpretation was one of the chief means to *fold the force* of a difficult reality.[17]

Despite hinting at the political potential of such practices, Foucault nevertheless retained a degree of ambivalence about these techniques of self. He was wary of the ways such practices could become institutionalized and therefore transformed into instrumental modes of managing human conduct. He made a point, for instance, of tracing the way several of these practices were eventually brought under the auspices of the Catholic Church through the more formalized practice of confession. He also retained his skepticism about psychoanalysis, regarding this form of therapeutic treatment as belonging to the long lineage of psychiatric methods in which an external authority seeks to manage the other's mind. Even as he explored the ancient techniques of self as a key site of ethics, Foucault remained vigilant about the way these practices could be transformed into rationalized modes for managing human conduct.[18]

Interpreting a dream, in this respect, is a risky business—yet another arena where power can be exercised over the other. And yet, as Foucault insisted, where there is power, there must be freedom. Even against the most profound exercises of power, there will be resistance: "At the very heart of the power relationship, and constantly provoking it, are the recalcitrance of the will and the intransigence of freedom."

Dreaming as Political Praxis

In dream-life, the particular agency responsible for folding the force of reality is the dream-work. If I may take the liberty of reminding the reader, this term refers to the operations of the mind that transform the latent dream-thoughts into the manifest content of the dream. This is a particular *form* of thought that does not operate according to the laws of rationality but rather possesses its own, unconscious logic. Freud identified four specific operations that together make up the dream-work—displacement, condensation, symbolization, and secondary elaboration—each of which effectively aims to transfigure the dream-thoughts, giving them a new form.

The raw materials of dream-life are shaped by each dreamer's unique lived context. Perhaps unsurprisingly, many of the dreams in Beradt's collection prominently feature banners and posters (often emblazoned with racially tinged slogans), speeches booming from loudspeakers, faceless storm troopers, as well as a variety of high-ranking Nazi politicians; Hitler, Göring, and Goebbels appeared so often in people's dreams, Beradt gave

them code names in her notes. While our dream-life inevitably works with
material derived from our particular environment—with what is situation-
ally given, so to speak—external forces do not dictate the dream-work's
particular labor of transformation, the way this material is *transfigured* in
the theater of the mind.

Freud privileged the operations of condensation and displacement,
often describing them as the *Werkmeisters* (or foremen) of the dream-
work, implying that these agents had the most power in the creation of the
dream. Ella Freeman Sharpe and Jacques Lacan both subsequently proposed that these particular operations could be fruitfully compared to
forms of poetic diction—metaphor and metonymy, in particular.[19] Freud,
on the other hand, tended to emphasize the visual dimensions of the
dream-work's transfigurations. In one striking passage of *The Interpretation of Dreams*, he provocatively compared the dream-work to composite
photography—the practice of superimposing two or more source images
to create one, combined image. While discussing his "R is my Uncle"
dream, he specifically mentions Francis Galton's visual experiments (at
Joseph Jacobs's request, Galton had attempted to produce a "Jewish type"
by superimposing a series of photographic portraits).[20] Here Freud provides a direct link between dream-work and contemporary visual practice.

The political stakes of this link would become more obvious in the
1920s, when the early experiments with composite photography gave way
to the avant-garde practice of montage. In the Soviet Union, El Lissitzky
and Aleksander Rodchenko fused the formal discoveries of constructivism
with the potential of photography to reach mass audiences. In Germany,
Dada artists such as John Heartfield and Hannah Höch used photomontage as a means to challenge the assumptions of bourgeois society. Montage was not only an innovative artistic technique; it also functioned as a
kind of symbolic form, a "shared visual idiom" that expressed the tumultuous arrival of urban-industrial life.[21] Montage, like the dream, is a visual
practice that presumes the truth is not given to sight but rather must be
actively deciphered. A series of compositional devices—some strikingly
similar to the operations of the dream-work—provide the means to bring
out this truth that has been obscured by political machination.

Consider John Heartfield's now iconic image from 1932, "The Meaning
of the Hitler Salute: Millions Are Standing Behind Me! Little Man Asks
for Big Gifts." The German artist-cum-political-dissident produced this
image for the popular *Workers' Illustrated Magazine* (*Die Arbeiter Illustrierte*

Zeitung, AIZ) where he worked. His tenure at the magazine enabled him to develop his characteristic style of cutting up and rearranging elements of contemporary press photographs, a method he compactly described with the slogan "Use photography as a weapon."[22] In "The Meaning of the Hitler Salute," Heartfield's parodies the leader's most iconic gesture through a dramatic difference in scale—an operation Freud might have identified as "displacement." The technique effectively resignifies the meaning of the salute, transforming the gesture into a symbol of Hitler's financial dependence on Germany's wealthy industrialists. Through this relatively simple juxtaposition, the image manages to paint the leader as a puppet of the industrial classes. In Heartfield's hands, displacement and condensation become potent visual devices that can expose the hidden alignments of power.

The techniques employed in montage can help to clarify the political significance of the dream-work. To return to Herr S's nightmare, recall that Beradt proposes that the central action of the manufacturer's dream—the struggle to raise his arm to salute Goebbels—is an experience that has been imposed from outside, as if Herr S's dream were a scene scripted and directed by the regime itself. In Beradt's mind, the nightmare is evidence of the profound reach of the Nazis' terrorism. Indeed, she positions the nightmare as an aspect of the terror itself.[23]

Such a view, however, cancels out the radical agency of the unconscious. Freud rightly insisted that a dream is an unconscious *production,* a complex mental event that has been carefully crafted using principles similar to montage. That is to say, the various operations of the dream-work reshape and recombine the raw materials drawn from daily life to give form to an unconscious thought. Herr S's dream is not just a documentary presentation of Nazi persecution but an active composition that works to *transvalue* the remains of the day. The architecture of dream-life is not something that is simply imprinted from the outside. A dream is a species of unconscious work that aims to make space for the creation of new symbolic meanings.[24] The creative aspect of this agency is perhaps most evident in Herr S's nightmare in the way the dreamer focuses on Goebbels's deformed foot. ("I was only able to keep from collapsing by staring at his clubfoot as he limped out.") The particular significance of this congenital deformity would need to be supplied through the dreamer's own associations, but the added detail does seem to turn the party's eugenic policies on their head, as if it were the minister himself who was the "degenerate."

John Heartfield, "The Meaning of the Hitler Salute: Little Man Asks for Big Gifts! Motto: Millions Stand Behind Me!" Photomontage. Cover of Arbeiter Illustrierte Zeitung (AIZ), October 1932. The Metropolitan Museum of Art, Purchase, The Horace W. Goldsmith Foundation Gift, through Joyce and Robert Menschel, 1987. Image copyright The Metropolitan Museum of Art. Image source: Art Resource, NY. Copyright The Heartfield Community of Heirs / SODRAC (2016).

In dark times, the techniques of dream-work can become potent weapons of dissent. These imaginary transfigurations offer evidence that even under the direst form of political oppression, the human being retains an inner capacity for resistance. Simply stated, dreaming serves as one of our most intimate instruments for refashioning reality.

The Zig-Zag Dream

Let me offer one last example in an effort to drive home the political stakes of this experimental action called dreaming. This final example is drawn from the life and work of the French philosopher Sarah Kofman. Kofman was born in Paris in 1934, and after a tumultuous wartime childhood, much of which was spent in hiding during the Nazi occupation, she eventually became professor of philosophy at the University of Paris I. Kofman was a prolific and innovative writer. Between 1970 and the time of her death in 1994 she published twenty-five books on a broad set of subjects. The question of the unconscious was one of the guiding threads throughout her productive career; she persistently returned to the crossing point between psychoanalysis, aesthetics, and literary criticism. Many commentators have noted the passion in her work—her acutely felt relationship to language and ideas. As an artist as well as a philosopher, Kofman possessed a complex and dramatic awareness of the way words and images work as tools of sense making. In her hands, these indispensible containers for meaning give form and shape to human experience, but they are also bearers of dense, existential dilemmas.

Kofman addressed some of these dilemmas directly in one of her last books, *Smothered Words* (*Paroles suffoquées*). The text engages the question of how one is able to write about Auschwitz, or rather how, after Auschwitz, one is still able to write at all. Working closely with Maurice Blanchot and Robert Antelme's work, Kofman espouses the view that no matter how vivid and stark a literary work might be, the comparison between a textual narrative and the lived experience of the camps can only be an insult to the actual horrors. Writing about Auschwitz will inevitably fail to do justice to the experience of Auschwitz. And yet despite this indignity, the philosopher insists on the ethical demand to write, indeed, to write precisely when one feels unable to do so: "To speak: it is necessary—*without (the) power* [*sans pouvoir*]: without allowing language, too powerful, sovereign,

to master the most aporetic situation, absolute powerlessness and very dis-
tress, to enclose it in the clarity and happiness of daylight."[25]

The project of trying to find a way to speak about the experience of
Auschwitz without emulsifying it in the light that language insists on shin-
ing upon its referents—to speak *without power*—was a task that was close
to Kofman's heart. In the summer of 1942, her father, Rabbi Berek Kofman,
was rounded up along with thirteen thousand other Parisian Jews, herded
into the city's winter velodrome and then dispatched to a camp at Drancy
to await deportation. Berek Kofman was eventually sent to Auschwitz,
where he survived for a little less than a year. According to a witness, on
one Sabbath day the rabbi refused to work and began to pray instead. He
was beseeching God "for all of them, victims and murderers alike," when
one of the Jewish kapos beat him to the ground with a pickax and then
buried him alive.[26]

Kofman first mentions her father's death in *Paroles suffoquées*. She does
not offer a narrative of his murder here—that is something that would
come later. Here she simply reports the historical facts drawn from the
memorial Serge Klarsfeld commissioned in Israel:

> Because he was a Jew, my father died in Auschwitz: How can it
> not be said? And how can it be said? How can one speak of that
> before which all possibility of speech ceases? Of this event, my
> absolute, which communicates with the absolute of history, and
> which is of interest only for this reason. . . . My father: Berek
> Kofman, born on October 10, 1900, in Sobin (Poland), taken to
> Drancy on July 16, 1942. Was in convoy no. 12, dated July 29, 1942,
> a convoy comprising 1,000 deportees, 270 men and 730 women
> (aged 36 to 54): 270 men registered 54,153 to 54,422; 514 women
> select for work, registered 13,320 to 13, 833; 216 other women gassed
> immediately.[27]

How to speak this? And yet how could she not speak of it? The sublime
"neutrality" of these facts can make one doubt common sense, indeed, all
sense. Kofman acutely grasps the way it seems impossible to create a story
from these facts, if by "story" one means: to generate a sequence of events
that makes sense. The brutal terms of Berek Kofman's death left his daughter suffocating in silence, wresting from her the very capacity to speak of
this "absolute" event of her life. One could describe this as an encounter

with the Real—an instance when something remains outside language, unassimilable, resisting symbolization, indeed, which only registers as a wrenching tear in the symbolic order, a breakdown in the human capacity to lend meaning and significance to events. The sheer force of such "facts" is perhaps beyond the capacity of any human being to both take in and remain fully, emotionally alive.

And yet Kofman knew that such events nevertheless demanded a narrative. This summons came, in part, from the imperative of those who did return *to tell,* indeed, to tell endlessly. Despite the smothering injunction, Kofman understood that one must find the means to speak, to find the means to speak precisely where one lacks the capacity to do so. Her deceptively simple, direct phrase—to speak *sans pouvoir*—suggests both an obligation to speak in situations where the capacity for speech is impossible, when speaking entails the very dissolution of the speaking subject, but also, and perhaps more importantly, to speak in a fashion that does not assume sovereign authority over the events—to speak in a way that protects the events from being emulsified by language, to protect the memory of her father's death from the further annihilating force of rationality.

A solution to this profound dilemma arrived in the form of a dream. The dream did not fully resolve the ethical quandary that Kofman (among others) had gone to lengths to describe. But it did provide a means to speak *without power;* it offered an alternative way to give voice to this absolute event, to represent her father's life and his death without striving make this narrative make sense.

The dream is reported early in *Rue Ordener, Rue Labat,* Kofman's last book, a slender and disarming memoir about her childhood under the Nazi occupation. "Later," she writes, "in a dream, my father appeared to me as a drunk zigzagging across the street."[28] The disclosure immediately follows Kofman's sparse account of her father's death in Auschwitz. Its positioning is crucial in this respect. Structurally speaking, it is not until "later," that is, *after* the dream, that Kofman was able to speak of this absolute event. One could say the dream *bent the force* of these events, serving both as catalyst and vehicle to voice what Toni Morrison named the "unspeakable things unspoken."[29]

I am hesitant to offer anything that resembles an interpretation of this achingly elegant dream, but Kofman herself presents readers with everything they need to grasp its significance. In the chapter of *Rue Ordener, Rue Labat* where the dream report appears, she describes her father's great love for and dependence on cigarettes. She tells us that the Sabbath rule against smoking was particularly difficult for him. The moment the day was over he would light one up. She fondly recalls how the family would spend the last hours of the day in his room, singing Hebrew songs and others with words her father made up. Years later, she recognized one of these melodies in a symphony by Gustav Mahler.[30] During the war, when tobacco was strictly rationed, she would collect butts from the sidewalk for him. It was her job to go to rue Jean-Robert to buy him the Zig-Zag papers he used to roll his cigarettes. After the Nazis took him away, the family received just one message from him, a note from Drancy, in which he asked for supplies, but "most of all, send cigarettes, blue or green Gauloises."[31] Through these delicate associations, Kofman gives her readers almost everything they need to know to understand the poignancy of her dream. She portrays her father as a man whose addiction to smoking made the Sabbath—the day he was murdered—an agony of withdrawal. She discloses how her father's addiction shaped the tender bond between father and daughter. Without needing to explain it, the reader can grasp how the quixotic dream-figure— her father as a drunk, zigzagging across the street—provided an unexpected return and re-presentation of otherwise unspeakable things. The dream managed to transfigure the absolute event of her life, allowing Kofman to draw breath and finds words, to escape its smothering force—to fold the force of an unbearable reality.

What else is a dream but a name for the inexplicable urge to speak of something that one has no power over, a kind of speaking *sans pouvoir*—a means to give voice to what is otherwise unspeakable? These thought-events manage to break open the speaking subject in a way that allows for a return to the knots in one's past where the heart is tied, knots that are often bound up with the absolutes of history. Perhaps dreaming is nothing more and nothing less than this: an unanticipated opening in thought and being, evidence of an indestructible alterity in each of us, an attestation to the fundamental human capacity to give form and shape to what is possible to say and think—in short, strange and enduring proof of the recalcitrance of the will and the intransigence of freedom.

Acknowledgments

I WAS FORTUNATE to have the opportunity to present early drafts of this project in several venues, including the political science department at Williams College, the history of art and visual culture department at the University of California, Santa Cruz, and the Faculty of Education at York University. The audiences in each of these places offered superb suggestions, many of which made their way into the book.

My editor, Pieter Martin, has been patient and supportive right from the beginning, when the idea for a book about the politics of dream-life was just a fleeting thought. Anne Carter, Danielle Kasprzak, and the rest of the team at the University of Minnesota Press made the production of the book a pleasure.

I would like to express my gratitude to the institutions that granted permission to reproduce the illustrations included in this book: the Nelson Mandela Centre of Memory, the Lee Miller Archives, the Bodleian Library, and the English department at the University of Oxford. My research was generously supported by the Social Science and Humanities Research Council of Canada.

My students have served as a constant wellspring. It is something of a truism to say that I can never return to them what they have given me. I have been further blessed with a magnanimous circle of friends and colleagues. I owe a great debt to Mark Reinhardt, who has been a generous interlocutor throughout the project and beyond. I also benefited enormously from conversation with Catherine Walker, the curator of the War Poets Collection at the Craiglockhart Campus of Edinburgh Napier University. Several of them read drafts, some patiently listened, and others kept me nourished, both in body and spirit. My sincere thanks goes to Deborah Britzman, Jenny Burman, David Clark, Alison Hearn, Keir Keightley, Gabby Moser, James Motluck, David Mutimer, Alice Pitt, Matthew Rowlinson,

Karyn Sandlos, Patricia Sliwinski, Shawn Michelle Smith, Daniela Snep-
pova, Sasha Torres, Sarah Whitaker, and Carol Zemel. A special thank-you
to Sarah Freke, for teaching me a great deal about dreams, but also for
patiently nurturing my questions about how to live.

My deepest gratitude to Melissa Adler, for so many things but in particular for managing to fashion the kind of relationship that Rilke once
dreamed about: two people who each stand guard over the solitude of the
other.

Notes

A Fairy for an Introduction

1. William Shakespeare, *Romeo and Juliet,* act 1, scene 4.

2. Christopher Bollas, *The Shadow of the Object: Psychoanalysis and the Unthought Known* (New York: Columbia University Press, 1987). Ella Freeman Sharpe similarly describes the dream as aiming to assimilate unconscious knowledge into consciousness, "the revelation of the unknown, implicit in the known." See Sharpe, *Dream Analysis* (London: Hogarth Press, 1959), 18.

3. See, for instance, Sigmund Freud, "Lecture XXIX: Revision of Dream-Theory," in *New Introductory Lectures on Psycho-Analysis* [1933], *The Standard Edition of the Complete Psychological Works of Sigmund Freud,* ed. and trans. James Strachey (London: Hogarth Press, 1953) (hereafter *SE*), 22:11.

4. Hannah Arendt, "Thinking and Moral Considerations" (1971), reprinted in *Responsibility and Judgment,* ed. Jerome Kohn (New York: Schocken Books, 2003), 189.

5. Hannah Arendt, "Freedom and Politics: A Lecture," *Chicago Review* 14, no. 1 (Spring 1960): 30. She also briefly discusses freedom in *The Human Condition* (Chicago: University of Chicago Press, 1998), 26.

6. Arendt, *The Human Condition,* 176. Arendt details three fundamental activities involved in the human condition: labor, work, and action. Labor is the ability to sustain human life, to meet our biological needs of consumption and reproduction. Work is the ability to build and maintain a world fit for human use. Action, which Arendt privileges, involves the disclosure of the identity of the actor. The aim of action is to reaffirm the reality of the world, to actualize the human capacity for freedom.

7. Ibid.

8. Jürgen Habermas, *The Theory of Communicative Action,* trans. Thomas McCarthy, vol. 1, *Reason and the Rationalization of Society* (Boston: Beacon Press, 1985). My argument leans on the idea—from Arendt as much as Habermas—that the public sphere is fashioned from communicative action, but my emphasis falls on the *unconscious* elements of communication.

9. Toni Morrison, "Unspeakable Things Unspoken: The Afro-American Presence in American Literature," Tanner Lecture on Human Values, delivered at the University of Michigan, October 7, 1998. Available online: http://tannerlectures .utah.edu/_documents/a-to-z/m/morrison90.pdf.

10. Arendt, *The Human Condition,* 175.

11. For more on Arendt's theory of storytelling as the grounds of politics, see Michael Jackson, *The Politics of Storytelling: Variations on a Theme By Hannah Arendt,* 2nd ed. (Chicago: University of Chicago Press, 2014).

12. Jacqueline Rose, *Women in Dark Times* (London: Bloomsbury, 2014), ix. There has been a long history of efforts to marry psychoanalysis and political theory. Specifically in relation to dream interpretation, the surrealists should be credited with initially moving the examination of dream-life out of its clinical and therapeutic context. The surrealists were also a catalyst for Walter Benjamin's unique brand of cultural history, which sought to construe the latent aspects of material culture. The discussion of Benjamin's methodology constitutes its own field; see, for example, Rolf Tiedemann, "Dialectics at a Standstill," in Walter Benjamin's *The Arcades Project,* ed. Rolf Tiedemann, trans. Howard Eiland and Kevin McLaughlin (Cambridge, Mass.: Belknap Press, 1999); Susan Buck-Morss, *The Dialectics of Seeing: Walter Benjamin and the Arcades Project* (Cambridge, Mass.: MIT Press, 1991); Jacques Derrida, *"Fichus*: Frankfurt Address," in *Paper Machine,* trans. Rachel Bowlby (Stanford, Calif.: Stanford University Press, 2005), 164–82; Tyrus Miller, "From City-Dreams to the Dreaming Collective: Walter Benjamin's Political Dream Interpretation," *Philosophy and Social Criticism* 22, no. 6 (1996): 87–111; and Helen Groth and Natalya Lusty, "'Dream Kitsch': Surrealism, Walter Benjamin and the Agency of the Dream," in *Dreams and Modernity: A Cultural History* (New York: Routledge, 2013), 121–47. Jonathan Lear has offered a different model for marrying dream interpretation and political philosophy in his book *Radical Hope: Ethics in the Face of Cultural Devastation* (Cambridge, Mass.: Harvard University Press, 2006).

13. Freud revised his terminology several times. In his 1923 paper "Das Ich und das Es," he introduced new terms that James Strachey translated into English as "the Ego" and "the Id"; *SE,* 19:1–63. Freud himself acknowledges borrowing his term *das Es* from Georg Groddeck, citing the precedent set by Nietzsche. As several commentators have pointed out, the more literal (and perhaps effective) translation of *das Es* is "the It."

14. Sarah Kofman, *Smothered Words,* trans. Madeline Dobie (Evanston, Ill.: Northwestern University Press, 1997), 10. I discuss Kofman's phrase in more detail in chapter 6.

15. A short list of texts in which Foucault investigates *parrhēsia* includes *Fearless Speech,* ed. Joseph Pearson (Los Angeles: Semiotext[e], 2001); *The Government of Self and Others: Lectures at the Collège de France, 1982–1983,* ed. Frédéric Gros,

trans. Graham Burchell (New York: Palgrave Macmillan, 2010); and *The Courage of Truth (The Government of Self and Others II): Lectures at the Collège de France, 1983–1984,* ed. Frédéric Gros, trans. Graham Burchell (New York: Palgrave Macmillan, 2011).

16. In the fall of 1980, Foucault visited a number of cities and universities in the United States. In 1981 he delivered a course of lectures at the Catholic University of Louvain. Together these lectures mark the transition in his work that I describe here: a shift from studying systems of power relations to studying techniques of critical agency. Transcripts of several of these lectures have been published; see, for instance, Michel Foucault, "About the Beginning of the Hermeneutics of the Self: Two Lectures at Dartmouth," *Political Theory* 21, no. 2 (May 1993): 198–227; and *Wrong-Doing, Truth-Telling: The Function of Avowal in Justice,* ed. Fabienne Brion and Bernard E. Harcourt, trans. Stephen W. Sawyer (Chicago: University of Chicago Press, 2014).

17. Foucault opened the third volume of his *History of Sexuality* trilogy with an extended analysis of the role of sexual dreams in Artemidorus's *Oneirocritica.* See *The History of Sexuality,* vol. 3, *The Care of the Self,* trans. Robert Hurley (New York: Vintage, 1988), 1–36.

18. Freud, *The Interpretation of Dreams* (1900), *SE,* 5:506 n. 2. Freud makes a similar point in "Remarks on the Theory and Practice of Dream-Interpretation" (1923), *SE,* 19:112; "History of the Psychoanalytic Movement" (1914), *SE,* 14:65; and "Some Neurotic Mechanisms" (1922), *SE,* 17:229.

19. Hannah Arendt, *Men in Dark Times* (New York: Harcourt Brace, 1968). As Arendt acknowledges, "dark times" is a phrase borrowed from Bertolt Brecht's poem "To Posterity." Scott Horton provides an original translation and discussion of Brecht's poem in *Harper's Blog.* Online (January 15, 2008): http://harpers.org/blog/2008/01/brecht-to-those-who-follow-in-our-wake. Arendt describes violence as "mute" in *The Human Condition,* 26. See also Roger Berkowitz, "Introduction: Thinking in Dark Times," in Roger Berkowitz, Jeffrey Katz, and Thomas Keenan, eds., *Thinking in Dark Times: Hannah Arendt on Ethics and Politics* (New York: Fordham University Press, 2010), 3–14.

20. Arendt, *Men in Dark Times,* viii.

21. David Grossman, *Writing in the Dark: Essays on Literature and Politics,* trans. Jessica Cohen (New York: Picador, 2009), 61. For more on the emptying out of human speech see Walter Benjamin, "The Story Teller: Observations on the Works of Nikolai Leskov" (1936), in *Selected Writings,* vol. 3, *1935–1938,* ed. Michael Jennings, trans. Marcus Bullock, Howard Eiland, and Gary Smith (Cambridge, Mass.: Belknap Press, 2002), 143–66; W. G. Sebald, "Air War and Literature," in *On the Natural History of Destruction* (New York: Hamish Hamilton, 1999); and Toni Morrison's Nobel Lecture, December 7, 1993, http://www.nobelprize.org/nobel_prizes/literature/laureates/1993/morrison-lecture.html.

22. Sigmund Freud, "Some Dreams of Descartes: A Letter to Maxime Leroy," *SE*, 21:203.

23. Broadly defined, "wild" analysis is when amateurs attempt to define dreams, symptoms, utterances, or actions using psychoanalytic concepts that they do not understand. Freud also used the term to refer to analytic interpretations that might be correct but that fail to heed the delicacy of the analytic situation, namely, the transference. Sándor Ferenczi described this as "compulsive analyzing." "Wild" can therefore refer to the ignorance of the interpreter, but it can also refer to the careless manner in which the interpretation is delivered. See Sigmund Freud, "'Wild' Analysis" (1910), *SE*, 11:221–27; Sándor Ferenczi, "The Elasticity of the Psycho-Analytic Technique," *Final Contributions to the Problems and Methods of Psycho-Analysis* (London: Hogarth Press, 1955), 98–99.

24. Sharpe, *Dream Analysis*, 14.

25. I am adapting the last of Walter Benjamin's thirteen theses of the writer's technique: "The work is the death mask of its conception." In *Reflections: Essays, Aphorisms, Autobiographical Writings,* ed. Peter Demetz, trans. Edmund Jephcott (New York: Schocken Books, 1986), 81.

26. Adrian Kohler, with contributions by Basil Jones and Tommy Luther, "Statement of Purpose: Handspring Puppet Company," *Journal of Modern Craft* 2, no. 3 (2009): 345–54.

27. William Kentridge, interview with Carolyn Christov-Bakargiev, in *William Kentridge* (London: Phaidon, 1999), 19.

28. I am also indebted here to Thomas Ogden's notion of the dream as an "intersubjective analytic event." Ogden argues that dreams dreamed in the course of an analysis should not be simply understood as belonging to the analysand. Rather they are a product generated by the interplay of the analyst, the analysand, and "the analytic third" (the "felt place" between the analyst and analysand). See Thomas Ogden, "The Analytic Third: Working with Intersubjective Clinical Facts," *International Journal of Psycho-Analysis* 75 (1994): 3–20; and "Dream Associations," in Ogden, *Reverie and Interpretation: Sensing Something Human* (London: Karnac, 1999): 135–54.

29. See Freud, "The Uncanny" (1919), *SE*, 17:217–56.

30. In his book-length essay, *S/Z*, Roland Barthes distinguishes between "readerly" and "writerly" texts. According to Barthes, most texts are readerly, which is to say, narratives that conform to standardized codes of style and content. Meaning is relatively fixed and the reader is put in the position of passively receiving the information contained therein. Writerly texts, in contrast, put control over the production of meaning into the reader's hands. These texts often disregard traditional narrative structure and invite a proliferation of meanings. Roland Barthes, *S/Z: An Essay,* trans. Richard Miller (New York: Hill and Wang, 1975).

1. The Prisoner's Defense

1. Mandela claims he uttered these words during a meeting he called with various local and foreign reporters after the three-day workers' stay-away had been crushed in May 1961. See *Long Walk to Freedom* (Boston: Little, Brown, 1994), 270. He said something similar during his first televised interview, which he gave to the British television network ITN around the same time. Available online: www.the atlantic.com/international/archive/2013/12/nelson-mandelas-first-tv-interview -may-1961/282120.

2. Mandela, *Long Walk to Freedom*, 390.

3. Ibid., 496.

4. Excerpts of Mandela's speech are reprinted in his autobiography and the complete text is available online: http://db.nelsonmandela.org/speeches/pub_ view.asp?pg=item&ItemID=NMS010. An audio recording is also available on the *Guardian's* website: http://www.theguardian.com/world/video/2013/dec/05/nel son-mandela-1964-speech-audio.

5. Sigmund Freud, *The Interpretation of Dreams* (1900), *SE*, 5:506 n. 2. Freud makes a similar point in "Remarks on the Theory and Practice of Dream-Interpretation" (1923), *SE*, 19:112; "History of the Psychoanalytic Movement" (1914), *SE*, 14:65; and "Some Neurotic Mechanisms" (1922), *SE*, 17:229.

6. Freud, *The Interpretation of Dreams*, *SE*, 4:48–50. Technically speaking, Freud calls the dream a "compromise formation," which is to say, it is the outcome of a conflict between a repressed idea or unconscious wish, and the ego's defensive demands for its censorship. Freud extended this notion of a compromise formation to apply to all products of the unconscious: dreams, symptoms, slips of the tongue, parapraxes, and so on. See chapter 23 of *The Introductory Lectures on Psycho-Analysis* (1916–17), *SE*, vol. 16.

7. Claude Lévi-Stauss discusses *bricolage* in *The Savage Mind,* trans. George Weidenfeld (London: Weidenfeld and Nicolson, 1966).

8. Mandela, *Long Walk to Freedom,* 570.

9. Reading psychoanalytically, negative statements are generally understood as taking cognizance of what is repressed. In his paper "Negation" (1925), Freud writes, "With the help of the symbol of negation, thinking frees itself from the restrictions of repression." *SE*, 19:239.

10. Franz Kafka, "The Metamorphosis," in *The Metamorphosis and Other Stories,* trans. Joyce Crick (Oxford: Oxford University Press, 2009), 29.

11. For a discussion of humanity and the gaze, see Hélène Cixous's "Volleys of Humanity," *Volleys of Humanity: Essays from 1972–2009* (Edinburgh: Edinburgh University Press, 2011), 264–85.

12. Freud, *The Interpretation of Dreams, SE,* 4:1.

13. For more on psychoanalysis as a critique of scientific reason see Léon Chertok and Isabelle Stengers, *A Critique of Psychoanalytic Reason: Hypnosis as a*

Scientific Problem from Lavoisier to Lacan, trans. Martha Noel Evans (Stanford, Calif.: Stanford University Press, 1992).

14. Jacqueline Rose, "Review of *What Is Madness* by Darian Leader," *Guardian,* October 1, 2011.

15. Arendt, *Between Past and Future: Eight Exercises in Political Thought* (New York: Penguin, 1968), 6. The Frankfurt School's absence in Arendt's narrative is noticeable. As Elisabeth Young-Bruehl has documented, Arendt carried a lifelong antipathy toward the Frankfurt Institute and to Theodor Adorno in particular. See Young-Bruehl's *Hannah Arendt: For the Love of the World,* 2nd ed. (New Haven, Conn.: Yale University Press, 2004), 80, 109, and 166–67.

16. Arendt, *Between Past and Future,* 8.

17. Ibid., 14.

18. Hannah Arendt, *Lectures on Kant's Political Philosophy,* ed. Ronald Beiner (Chicago: University of Chicago Press, 1992).

19. Immanuel Kant, *The Critique of Judgment,* trans. James Creed Meredith (Oxford: Oxford University Press, 1957), 152. The other two maxims include the ability to think for oneself and the ability to think consistently.

20. Maya Angelou, "His Day Is Done," in *The Complete Poetry* (New York: Random House, 2015), 306.

21. See Rita Barnard's introduction to *The Cambridge Companion to Nelson Mandela* (New York: Cambridge University Press, 2014), 3.

22. Mandela, *Long Walk to Freedom,* 624–25.

23. Hannah Arendt, *Between Past and Future,* 146.

24. Wilfred Bion, *Learning from Experience* (London: Karnac, 1962), 8. Bion greatly expanded Freud's axiomatic claim that dreams were simply another *form* of thought. A British doctor who served in the First World War and trained at the Tavistock Clinic, Bion proposed that dreaming is called into existence to cope with disturbing thoughts both in sleep and in unconscious waking life. He introduced the term *alpha-function* to refer to the mental process that transforms raw sense-impressions related to emotional experience into useable elements that can be linked with one another in the process of conscious and unconscious thinking and dreaming. Bion's extension and adaptation of Freud's theory of dreaming is often described as a paradigm shift in psychoanalytic theory. His theory of "alpha-functioning" bears strong similarities to Freud's model of dream-work, but Bion felt that psychoanalytic terminology had become so saturated with associations that it was necessary to invent new terms to generate fresh thinking. Bion defines alpha-functioning as the process of digesting the emotional encounter with "beta-elements" (i.e., raw sense impressions), into "alpha elements" (emotional material that can be stored in memory and made accessible for linking). If the beta-elements prove to be too emotionally disturbing—indigestible, to follow Bion's metaphor—alpha-functioning can be disturbed. For more on Bion's adaptation of

Freud's model of dreaming, see Thomas Ogden, "On Not Being Able to Dream," *International Journal of Psychoanalysis* 84 (2003): 17–30; James Grotstein, "Dreaming as a 'Curtain of Illusion': Revisiting the 'Royal Road' with Bion as Our Guide," *International Journal of Psychoanalysis* 90 (2009): 733–52; John A. Schneider, "From Freud's Dream-Work to Bion's Work of Dreaming: The Changing Conception of Dreaming in Psychoanalytic Theory," *International Journal of Psychoanalysis* 91 (2010): 521–40; and Michael Eigan, *Damaged Bonds* (London: Karnac, 2001).

25. Arendt, *Between Past and Future*, 156.

26. Mandela, *Long Walk to Freedom*, 623.

27. D. W. Winnicott, "Thinking and the Unconscious" (originally published in the *Liberal*, March 1945), republished in *Home Is Where We Start From* (New York: W. W. Norton, 1990), 169.

28. André Green, "Psychoanalysis and Ordinary Modes of Thought," in *On Private Madness* (London: Karnac, 1997), 18.

29. Freud, *The Interpretation of Dreams, SE*, 5:506.

30. Freud, *The Interpretation of Dreams, SE*, 4:311–12.

31. Readers of Freud will recognize that my terminology does not match what is set out in *The Interpretation of Dreams*. Freud himself described the four mechanisms of the dream: *Verdichtung* (condensation), *Verschiebung* (displacement), *Rücksicht auf Darstellbarkeit* (considerations of representability), and *sekundäre Bearbeitung* (secondary revision). He consistently revised these terms and subsequent analysts have further modified his language. Like many, I follow Ella Freeman Sharpe's modification. See her short, brilliant study, *Dream Analysis*, 13.

32. Freud, *The Interpretation of Dreams, SE*, 5:507. In "Remarks on the Theory and Practice of Dream Interpretation" (1923), he also warns analysts against the lure of trying to uncover the latent content at the expense of attending to the dream-work, the particular formal transformations that the dream performs. *SE*, 19:112.

33. Sigmund Freud, *The Interpretation of Dreams, SE*, 5:506 n. 2. Freud makes a similar point in "Remarks on the Theory and Practice of Dream-Interpretation," *SE*, 19:112; "History of the Psychoanalytic Movement" (1914), *SE*, 14:65; and "Some Neurotic Mechanisms" (1922), *SE*, 17:229.

34. Mandela, *Long Walk to Freedom*, 135.

35. Of course, totalitarian governments have always found various ways to "disappear" individuals and groups that are deemed undesirable, whether through purification laws (such as the racial policies in Nazi Germany) or individually targeted political exile (such as Madame Germaine de Staël's banishment from France during Napoleon's reign).

36. Robert L. Miller, "From the Publisher," *Time*, February 5, 1990, 10. An unattributed photograph from the 1960s showing Mandela repairing his prison clothes

while still incarcerated on Robben Island is prominently featured in the accompanying article.

37. Jenny Edkins, *Face Politics* (London: Routledge, 2015).

38. Mandela, *Long Walk to Freedom*, 144.

39. See Giorgio Agamben, *Homo Sacer: Sovereign Power and Bare Life*, trans. Daniel Heller-Roazen (Stanford, Calif.: Stanford University Press, 1998); Jacques Derrida, "The Force of Law: 'The Mystical Foundation of Authority,'" *Cardozo Law Review* 11 (1990): 920–1046; *The Beast and the Sovereign*, vols. 1 and 2, ed. Michel Lisse, Marie-Louise Mallet, and Ginette Michaud, trans. Geoffrey Bennington (Chicago: University of Chicago Press, 2009, 2011). It is tempting to argue that Derrida's work on sovereignty and the force of law stems directly from his admiration for Mandela. Although rarely cited, Derrida (together with Mustapha Tlili) edited a collection of writings and tributes simply titled *For Nelson Mandela*, which was first published in France in 1986—shortly before the more familiar theoretical investigations named above. Derrida contributed a long essay to the volume called "The Laws of Reflection: Nelson Mandela, in Admiration," in which he begins reflecting on the work of justice and its relationship to the law. See *For Nelson Mandela* (New York: Seaver Books, 1987), 11–42.

40. In *Truth and Method,* Hans-Georg Gadamer outlines how the noun *Erlebnis,* in the first instance, means "to be alive when something happens," and thus speaks to the sense of proximity and immediacy—something that one has experienced for oneself. But the form *das Erlebte* also refers to a sense of sustained insight that is achieved as a result of the immediate experience: "Something becomes an 'experience' not only insofar as it is experienced, but insofar as its being experienced makes a special impression that gives it lasting importance."

Erlebnis, therefore, refers to a kind of defining moment, an exceptional experience that is nevertheless tied to the everyday, which in turn is folded back to fertilize a larger, historical understanding of a life. Phenomenologists privilege this category of lived experience because it captures a sense of immediacy that precedes the more rationalized processes of description. See Hans-Georg Gadamer, *Truth and Method,* trans. Joel Weinsheimer and Donald G. Marshall (London: Bloomsbury, 2004), 55–56.

41. Christopher Bollas's term, the "unthought known," refers to unconscious knowledge that is not emotionally digested enough to be consciously "thought." See Bollas's *The Shadow of the Object.*

42. Didier Anzieu, *The Skin Ego: A Psychoanalytic Approach to Self,* trans. Chris Turner (New Haven, Conn.: Yale University Press, 1989). As I mentioned earlier, I am condensing a particular strand of psychoanalytic theory that has theorized dream-work as a process of thinking that is akin to "working through." This approach modifies Freud's thinking about symbolization. While Freud had a somewhat rigid sense of symbol formation—he imagined a constancy of the relationship

between the symbol and what it represents—later analysts emphasize *symbolic function*: what the particular *use* of the symbol allows in terms of psychological development.

43. Hanna Segal wrote extensively on the subject of dreaming and symbol formation. Two important papers include "Notes on Symbol Formation" (1957) and "The Function of Dreams" (1981), both reprinted in *The Work of Hanna Segal: A Kleinian Approach to Clinical Practice* (London: Free Association Books, 1986). For more on damaged dream-work see chapter 3 of Michael Eigan's *Damaged Bonds*, 43–61.

44. Mandela, *Conversations with Myself* (New York: Farrar, Straus and Giroux, 2010).

45. Freud elaborated his thoughts about the function of words as a complex presentation that combines auditory, visual, and kinaesthetic elements in appendix C of "The Unconscious" (1915), *SE*, 14:209–15.

46. See Sándor Ferenczi, "To Whom Does One Relate One's Dream?" (1912) and "Dreams of the Unsuspecting" (1916–17), both reprinted in *Further Contributions to the Theory and Technique of Psycho-analysis* (London: Hogarth Press, 1950).

47. Masud Khan, "The Use and Abuse of Dream in Psychic Experience" (1972), reprinted in *The Privacy of the Self* (New York: International Universities Press, 1974), 306–15.

48. J.-B. Pontalis, *Frontiers in Psychoanalysis: Between the Dream and Psychic Pain,* trans. Catherine Cullen and Philip Cullen (London: Hogarth Press, 1981), 28.

49. Sigmund Freud, *The Interpretation of Dreams, SE,* 4: xxiii–iv.

50. Khan, "Dream Psychology and the Evolution of the Psychoanalytic Situation" (1962) and "The Use and Abuse of Dream in Psychic Experience," both reprinted in *The Privacy of the Self,* and "The Changing Use of Dreams in Psychoanalytic Practice: In Search of the Dreaming Experience," *International Journal of Psychoanalysis* 57 (1976): 325–30.

51. Khan, "The Use and Abuse of Dream in Psychic Experience," in *The Privacy of the Self,* 314.

52. Khan, "The Changing Use of Dreams in Psychoanalytic Practice," 328.

53. Pontalis, *Frontiers in Psychoanalysis,* 33.

54. Ibid., 37.

55. Mandela, *Long Walk to Freedom,* 496–97.

56. J. L. Austin, *How to Do Things with Words* (Cambridge, Mass.: Harvard University Press, 1962).

57. The Defiance Campaign against Unjust Laws was presented by the ANC at a conference held in Bloemfontein, South Africa, in December 1951. During the conference the ANC and the Indian Congress drafted a public statement about the principles of the Defiance Campaign. The full report is available online: http://vi

.sahistory.org.za/pages/library-resources/articles_papers/karis-cartervol2/docu
ment86.htm.

58. Jean-Luc Nancy, *The Experience of Freedom*, trans. Bridget McDonald
(Stanford, Calif.: Stanford University Press, 1993), 8.

59. Mandela, *Conversations with Myself*, 350.

60. Verne Harris, introduction to ibid., xv.

61. Philip Holden, *Autobiography and Decolonization: Modernity, Masculinity,
and the Nation-State* (Madison: University of Wisconsin Press, 2008).

62. Among other places, Freud discusses secondary revision in *The Interpretation of Dreams, SE*, 5:488–508, and in *Totem and Taboo, SE*, 13:95. The extent of this
particular revision remains a question. In a recorded conversation Mandela had
with Richard Stengel during the preparation of the autobiography, Mandela
denies having had any recurring dreams in prison:

> STENGEL: Did you have recurring nightmares when you were on Robben
> Island?
>
> MANDELA: No, no, no. That I never had.
>
> STENGEL: Oh, you didn't, okay.
>
> MANDELA: No, I never had nightmares. (*Conversations with Myself*, 191)

It is difficult to know whether Mandela is simply contradicting himself here, or
if the recurring nightmare reported in *Long Walk to Freedom* is in fact a composite
(or outright invention) based on the many dreams Madiba *did* record—including
a similar dream he described for Winnie in a letter in 1976 (see the text accompanying note 55). I queried the Mandela Foundation, but they do not have a manuscript copy of this recurring dream among the records.

63. Richard Stengel, *Mandela's Way: Lessons on Life, Love, and Courage* (New
York: Crown Publishers, 2010), 16. See also Nadine Gordimer, *Living in Hope
and History* (London: Bloomsbury, 1999); and Daniel Roux, "Mandela Writing/
Writing Mandela," in *The Cambridge Companion to Nelson Mandela*, 205–23.

64. Shortly before his death in 1984, Foucault spoke of an idea for a new book
on "technologies of the self." He gave several lectures on the topic, including
a seminar presented at the University of Vermont in the fall of 1982. A partial
record of the seminar is published in *Technologies of the Self: A Seminar with Michel
Foucault*, ed. Luther H. Martin, Huck Gutman, and Patrick H. Hutton (London:
Tavistock, 1988).

65. Michel Foucault, "The Ethics of the Concern of the Self as a Practice of
Freedom," in *Ethics: Subjectivity and Truth*, ed. Paul Rabinow, trans. Robert Hurley
et al. (New York: New Press, 1997), 283–84.

66. Mandela, *Long Walk to Freedom*, 624–25.

67. Achilles Tatius, *The Adventures of Leucippe and Clitophon*, cited in Michel
Foucault, *The Care of the Self*, vol. 3 of *The History of Sexuality*, trans. Robert Hurley
(New York: Vintage, 1988), 5.

68. Foucault, *The Care of the Self*, 35.

69. Mandela kept a series of desk calendars on Robben Island and in Polls-moor and Victor Verster Prisons that run from 1976 to 1989. These particular entries are reprinted in *Conversations with Myself*, 267–68. "Zindzi" refers to one of Mandela's daughters (from his second marriage, to Winnie Madikizela), and "Kgatho" is one of Mandela's sons (from his first marriage, to Evelyn Mase). The calendars and other items can be viewed at the Nelson Mandela Centre of Memory: www.archive.nelsonmadela.org.

70. Arendt, *Men in Dark Times*, viii. See note 19 in Introduction. Scott Horton provides an original translation and discussion of Brecht's poem in *Harper's Blog* (January 15, 2008): http://harpers.org/blog/2008/01/brecht-to-those-who-follow -in-our-wake.

2. The Mother's Defense

1. Sigmund Freud, *The Interpretation of Dreams, SE*, 4:154–55.

2. Freud, *The Interpretation of Dreams, SE*, 4:249.

3. Ibid.

4. Ibid.

5. Ibid.

6. J.-B. Pontalis, *Frontiers in Psychoanalysis*, 40.

7. Freud, *Introductory Lectures on Psycho-Analysis* (1916–17 [1915–17]), *SE*, 15:5, 202. Freud taught at the university from about 1885 until 1916, and it seems entirely possible that he regularly presented Frau K's dream in this manner, although no record of these earlier lectures remain.

8. If, as it is often remarked, Freud neglected to pay much attention to the role of the mother, this figure has become a dominant subject of subsequent generations of psychoanalytic thinking. Melanie Klein focused much of her work on the child's earliest experiences of the mother. D. W. Winnicott offered the notion of the "good enough mother," and Wilfred Bion based his theory of the contained/container on the model of the mother's capacity to make sense of what is going on inside the infant. More recently, Julia Kristeva has focused on the mother's own experience, and specifically on what she names the "passion of motherhood," as a way to emphasize the intensity of the bond.

9. Wilfred Owen, "The Parable of the Old Man and the Young," in *The Collected Poems of Wilfred Owen*, ed. C. Day Lewis (New York: Chatto and Windus, 1963), 43.

10. I am referring here to the specific operation of the dream-work that Freud named *Rücksicht auf Darstellbarkeit*, or what James Strachey translated as "considerations of representability." In English, this awkward phrase has been replaced with "symbolization" in Hanna Segal's work among others. See Segal's *Dreams*,

Phantasy and Art (New York: Routledge, 1991). In the French literature, Freud's *Darstellbarkeit* was initially translated as *figurabilité*; this concept has seen a parallel elaboration in the literature, and has been recently retranslated into English as the neologism "figurability." See César Botella and Sára Botella, *The Work of Psychic Figurability: Mental Spaces without Representation*, trans. Andrew Weller (New York: Brunner-Routledge, 2005).

11. Alice Pitt, "Mother Love's Education," in *Love's Return: Psychoanalytic Essays on Childhood, Teaching, and Learning*, ed. Gail Masuchika Boldt and Paula M. Salvio (London: Taylor & Francis, 2006), 87.

12. See Nicole Loraux, *Mothers in Mourning*, trans. Corrine Pache (Ithaca, N.Y.: Cornell University Press, 1998) 51.

13. Foucault, *The Government of Self and Others*.

14. Ibid., 105.

15. H.D., *Hippolytus Temporizes & Ion* (New York: New Directions, 2003), 171.

16. There is another layer of this conflict built into the play: as Queen of Athens, Kreousa is a descendant of Erechtheus, the archaic king and founder of Athens, who himself was motherless—"earth begot" as Ion puts it.

17. This is H.D.'s translation, although I've modified her line breaks. See *Hippolytus Temporizes & Ion*, 209–13.

18. Foucault, *The Government of Self and Others*, 154.

19. United Nations International Criminal Tribunal for the former Yugoslavia, testimony of Witness 87 in the case against Kunarac, Kovač, and Vuković. Available online: www.icty.org/sid/10117.

20. Jacques Lacan, "The Instance of the Letter in the Unconscious, or Reason Since Freud," in *Écrits: The First Complete Edition in English*, trans. Bruce Fink (New York: W. W. Norton, 2006), 438.

21. The idea that the psychoanalytic process should serve as an analogue of the dreaming function has a long lineage that includes (although this is by no means an exhaustive list) Masud R. Khan, "Dream Psychology and the Evolution of the Psychoanalytic Situation," *International Journal of Psycho-Analysis* 43 (1962): 21–31; Khan, "The Use and Abuse of Dream in Psychic Experience"; and Khan, "The Changing Use of Dreams in Psychoanalytic Practice." See also J.-B. Pontalis, "The Dream as an Object," *International Review of Psycho-Analysis* 1 (1974): 125–33; Hanna Segal, "Notes on Symbol Formation" and "The Function of Dreams," in *The Work of Hanna Segal*, 49–65 and 89–97, respectively; Thomas Ogden, "This Art of Psychoanalysis: Dreaming Undreamt Dreams and Uninterrupted Cries," *International Journal of Psycho-Analysis* 85 (2004): 857–77; Ogden, "On Holding and Containing, Being and Dreaming," *International Journal of Psycho-Analysis* 85 (2004): 1349–64.

22. Arendt, *The Human Condition*, 176; emphasis added.

23. Hannah Arendt, *The Life of the Mind* (San Diego: Harcourt, 1978), 217.

24. Freud himself hints at the relationship between dreaming and the maternal function (or at least the fact of natality) during the analysis of his specimen dream. In musing on the various women the dream evokes, he notes, "There is at least one spot in every dream at which it is unplumbable—a navel, as it were, that is its point of contact with the unknown." *The Interpretation of Dreams*, 111 n. 1. Strikingly, he marks the dream's vanishing point not with the proverbial "x" but rather with "the navel"—that odd vestige of the umbilical cord, the organ that once physically connected us to our mother's body. Picking up on the passage, J.-B. Pontalis has speculated that "every dream, as an object of analysis, refers to the maternal body." See *Frontiers of Psychoanalysis*, 29. Wilfred Bion extended this insight further with his concept of the "container," which refers both to the mother's capacity for reverie and the dreaming function. See *Learning from Experience*.

25. Hannah Arendt, "Truth and Politics," *New Yorker*, February 25, 1967, 49.

3. The Soldier's Defense

1. Cecil Day Lewis, introduction to *The Collected Poems of Wilfred Owen* (New York: Chatto and Windus, 1963), 1.

2. Wilfred Owen, "Strange Meeting"; Owen composed the poem in 1918 and it was unpublished in his lifetime; *Collected Poems*, 35. Owen also uses the phrase the "Pity of War" in his preface to a planned collection of his war poetry.

3. John Keats, letter to George and Thomas Keats, 21 December 1817, in *The Complete Poetical Works and Letters of John Keats, Cambridge Edition* (Boston: Houghton Mifflin, 1899), 277. Like Owen's "pity of war," Keats's "Negative Capability" has come to be used in many contexts, some of which bend it very far from its original meaning. See Li Ou, *Keats and Negative Capability* (New York: Continuum, 2009).

4. Hibberd notes Henry Newbolt's initial review, which dismissed Owen's poetry as the work of a "broken man." Dominic Hibberd, *Wilfred Owen: A New Biography* (Chicago: Ivan R. Dee, 2003), 243.

5. Arendt, "What Is Freedom?," in *Between Past and Future*, 156.

6. Arendt, *The Human Condition*, 186. Emphasis added.

7. Ibid., 186–87. Emphasis added.

8. James Dao and Andrew W. Lehren, "Baffling Rise in Suicides Plague Military," *New York Times*, May 15, 2013.

9. On suicide as a symbolic act, see Slavoj Žižek, *Enjoy Your Symptom! Jacques Lacan in Hollywood and Out* (London: Routledge, 1992), 43–44.

10. Wilfred Owen, letter #505, to Susan Owen, 25 April 1917, *Wilfred Owen: Selected Letters*, ed. John Bell (Oxford: Oxford University Press, 1985), 238.

11. Owen, letter #508, to Mary Owen, 8 May 1917, ibid., 242.

12. This is based on Hibberd's interpretation of Owen's cryptic account. See Hibberd, *Wilfred Owen,* 240.

13. Medical Board Report, 25 June 1917, from Owen's army file. Cited in ibid., 242. In light of recent medical research, it is perhaps important to add that Owen suffered a concussion shortly before the incident at the railway embankment. In March 1917, while searching for a sick man in the dark, Owen fell into a fifteen-foot hole, hitting the back of his head on the way down. He was entombed there for more than a day, but the doctors diagnosed him with a slight concussion and deemed him fit for duty. Shortly afterward, however, he suddenly became violently sick. As his biographer, Dominic Hibberd, has suggested, with hindsight, one can see this fall as the beginning of his neurasthenia. This story seems to add evidence to the small group of contemporary military researchers who have recently argued that PTSD is, in fact, a largely physical condition—a species of brain degeneration called chronic traumatic encephalopathy, which can be caused by exposure to a blast or a severe concussion (both of which Owen suffered). See Shively et al., "Characterisation of Interface Astroglial Scarring in the Human Brain after Blast Exposure: A Post-mortem Case Series," *Lancet Neurology* 15, no. 9 (2016): 944–53; Robert F. Worth, "What if PSTD Is More Physical than Psychological?," *New York Times Magazine,* June 10, 2016, http://www.nytimes.com/2016/06/12/magazine/what-if-ptsd-is-more-physical-than-psychological.html.

14. Owen, letter #506, to Susan Owen, 2 May 1917, *Wilfred Owen: Selected Letters,* 240.

15. See Douglas Kerr's chapter on "Susan" in *Wilfred Owen's Voices* (Oxford: Clarendon Press, 1993), 48–64.

16. In later editions of *Good-Bye to All That,* the statement was modified to "unjustly accused." As Owen's biographer notes, the question of Wilfred's alleged cowardice has "a long history of being suppressed, skated over, forgotten or, much less often, wildly exaggerated." See Dominic Hibberd, "Appendix B: The Accusation of Cowardice," *Wilfred Owen,* 374–75.

17. Ted Bogacz, "War Neurosis and Cultural Change in England, 1914–1922: The Work of the War Office Committee of Enquiry in 'Shell-Shock,'" *Journal of Contemporary History* 24, no. 2 (April 1989): 228.

18. Bogacz cites Lord Southborough's remark from his speech in support of the motion for the Enquiry in the House of Lords in ibid. See also David Sharp "Shocked, Shot, and Pardoned," *Lancet* 368, no. 9540 (16 September 2006): 975–76.

19. Wyndham Lewis, *Men without Art,* in Julian Symons, ed., *The Essential Wyndham Lewis* (London: Andre Deutsch, 1989), 211.

20. William Shakespeare, *Romeo and Juliet,* act 1, scene 4, lines 81–82.

21. See Marc-Antoine Croq and Louis Croq, "From Shell Shock and War Neurosis to Post-traumatic Stress Disorder: A History of Psychotraumatology," *Dialogues in Clinical Neuroscience* 2, no. 1 (2000): 47–55.

22. From David Worthington's poem "Waterloo." Available online: http://www .waterloo200.org/waterloo-a-poem-by-david-worthington. Nicholas Boyle offers an account of how Goethe was curious to experience "cannon fever" for himself and rode into the front at the Battle of Valmy. See *Goethe: The Poet and the Age,* vol. 2, *Revolution and Renunciation* (Oxford: Oxford University Press, 2000), 127.

23. For an overview of these debates see Edgar Jones and Simon Wessely, *Shell Shock to PTSD: Military Psychiatry from 1900 to the Gulf War* (New York: Taylor and Francis, 2005).

24. Charles Myers, "A Contribution to the Study of Shell Shock: Being an Account of Three Cases of Loss of Memory, Vision, Smell, and Taste, Admitted into the Duchess of Westminster's War Hospital, Le Tourqet," *Lancet,* February 13, 1915, 316–20. Myers published three more papers on shell shock in 1916, although he was not the first to coin the term "shell shock." According to Merskey and Brown, the first mention of the term appears to have been in a story published in the *Times* on February 6, 1915, which described the War Office's arrangements to send soldiers suffering from "shock" to be treated in special wards at the National Hospital for the Paralysed and Epileptic in Queen Square. See Harold Merskey and Edward Brown, "Post-traumatic Stress Disorder and Shell Shock," in German Berrios and Roy Porter, eds., *A History of Clinical Psychiatry* (London: Athlone Press, 1995), 490–500.

25. Cited in Bernd Ulrich and Benjamin Ziemann, *Frontalltag im Ersten Weltkrieg: Wahn und Wirklichkeit* (Frankfurt: Fischer. 1994), 102–3.

26. Available online, through British Pathé: http://www.britishpathe.com/ workspaces/BritishPathe/shell-shock. It should be noted that this footage was shot to document the condition but also to promote Hurst's method of treatment. The reels were structured in before-and-after segments that were designed to advertise the success of the doctor's method.

27. "The new wounded" is Catherine Malabou's phrase for a category of wounding that she argues lies between psychopathology and brain damage, a kind of "cerebrality," as she puts it, in which cerebral events coincide with psychic events. Malabou, *The New Wounded: From Neurosis to Brain Damage,* trans. Steven Miller (New York: Fordham University Press, 2012).

28. During this period of industrialization, railway accidents were becoming more and more common. Survivors who showed no physical injuries often displayed symptoms that were typical of what today is called post-traumatic stress disorder. Soon these survivors started petitioning the railroads for compensation; the railroads in turn rejected the claims as fake. In 1884 the chancellor of Germany, Otto von Bismarck, passed accident insurance legislation that legally guaranteed financial compensation to survivors. Debate raged in medical circles as to the etiology: Germany's leading neurologist, Hermann Oppenheim, claimed that railway spine was due to physical damage to the spine or brain, whereas French

neurologist Jean-Martin Charcot diagnosed the condition as a variant of hysteria. See Paul Lerner, "Psychiatry and Casualties of War in Germany, 1914–1918," *Journal of Contemporary History* 35, no. 1 (2000): 13–28; and Claudie Massicotte, "Mapping Memory through the Railway Network: Reconsidering Freud's Metaphors," in Steven D. Spalding and Benjamin Fraser, eds., *Trains, Literature, and Culture: Reading and Writing the Rails* (Plymouth, UK: Lexington Books, 2012), 159–78.

29. Ernst Simmel, "War Neurosis and 'Psychic Trauma'" ["Kriegs-Neurosen und 'Psychisches Trauma'" (1918)], in Anton Kaes, Martin Jay, and Edward Dimendberg, eds., *The Weimar Republic Sourcebook* (Berkeley: University of California Press, 1995), 7.

30. E. D. Adrian and L. R. Yealland, "The Treatment of Some Common War Neuroses," *Lancet,* June 9, 1917, 865.

31. Ibid,, 869.

32. Lewis Yealland, *Hysterical Disorders of Warfare* (London: Macmillan, 1918), 7–15.

33. For a discussion of the Wagner-Jauregg investigation see M. S. Gunther, ed., "Freud as Expert Witness: Wagner-Jauregg and the Problem of War Neuroses," *Annual of Psychoanalysis,* vol. 2 (New York: International Universities Press, 1974), 4–22; and K. R. Eissler, *Freud as an Expert Witness: The Discussion of the War Neuroses between Freud and Wagner-Jauregg,* trans. Christine Trollope (Madison, Conn.: International Universities Press, 1986).

34. Sigmund Freud, "Memorandum on the Electrical Treatment of War Neurotics" (1920), *SE,* 17:211–16.

35. Sigmund Freud, citied in Eissler, *Freud as an Expert Witness,* 60–61.

36. Ibid.. 72.

37. Ibid., 64. These plans did take shape in the Berlin Psychoanalytic Polyclinic, which offered free treatment to the public. See Elizabeth Ann Danto, *Freud's Free Clinics: Psychoanalysis and Social Justice, 1918–1938* (New York: Columbia University Press, 2005).

38. Freud, citied in Eissler, *Freud as an Expert Witness,* 62.

39. Craiglockhart War Hospital, SS7/1, unidentified notes, Siegfried Sassoon papers (ref P444), Department of Documents, Imperial War Museum, London.

40. Arthur J. Brock, "Re-education of the Adult: The Neurasthenic in War and Peace," *Sociological Review* 10 (1918), 29, emphasis in the original, and 31.

41. For more on Dr. Arthur Brock's method and its influence on Wilfred Owen, see David Cantor, "Between Galen, Geddes, and the Gael: Arthur Brock, Modernity, and Medical Humanism in Early-Twentieth-Century Scotland," *Journal of the History of Medicine and Allied Sciences* 60, no. 1 (January 2005): 1–41; and Dominic Hibberd, "A Sociological Cure for Shellshock: Dr. Brock and Wilfred Owen," *Sociological Review* 25, no. 2 (May 1977): 377–86.

42. Brock published a short piece about Antaeus in the *Hydra*, a journal that was produced by the soldiers at Craiglockhart and that Wilfred Owen edited during his time there: Arthur J. Brock, "Antaeus, or Back to the Land," *Hydra*, no. 3 (January 1918): 3–4.

43. Arthur J. Brock, *Health and Conduct* (London: Le Play House, 1923), 171–72. Emphasis in the original. Brock's book was published just three years after Sassoon published the first collection of Owen's poetry in 1920.

44. Owen, *Collected Poems*, 55.

45. Owen, letter #552, to Susan Owen, Tuesday [16 October, 1917?], *Wilfred Owen: Selected Letters*, 283.

46. I am borrowing from Douglas Kerr's argument in *Wilfred Owen's Voices: Language and Community* (Oxford: Clarendon Press, 1993), 60.

47. Sigmund Freud, *Beyond the Pleasure Principle* (1920), *SE*, 18:13.

48. Philip Gourevitch and Errol Morris, "Annals of War: Exposure," *New Yorker*, March 24, 2008. Online: http://www.newyorker.com/reporting/2008/03/24/080324fa_fact_gourevitch.

49. Ibid., n.p.

50. Wilfred Owen, "Strange Meeting," *Collected Poems*, 35.

4. The Artist's Defense

1. Edward R. Murrow, *This Is London*, ed. Elmer Davis (New York: Simon and Schuster, 1941), 140.

2. Ibid., 146 and 167.

3. Ibid., 172–73.

4. Giulio Douhet, *The Command of the Air*, trans. Dino Ferrari (London: Faber and Faber, 1943), 14.

5. Walter Benjamin, "The Story Teller: Observations on the Works of Nikolai Leskov" (1936), in *Selected Writings*, vol. 3, *1935–1938*, 144.

6. W. G. Sebald, "Air War and Literature," 10–11, emphasis added. Of all the German literary works written at the end of the 1940s, Sebald finds only two that dared to face the horror of the ruins: Heinrich Böll's *Der Engel schwieg* (*The Silent Angel*) and Hans Erich Nossack's *Der Untergang: Hamburg 1943* (*The End: Hamburg 1943*).

7. In *The Childhood of Art: An Interpretation of Freud's Aesthetics*, trans. Winifred Woodhull (New York: Columbia University Press, 1988), Sarah Kofman characterizes dream as the paradigm of the work of art and argues that Freud's method of interpreting dreams is borrowed from the interpretation of art. Visual and literary symbolism corroborates the symbolism of dreams, which is to say, Kofman suggests that Freud's theory is more indebted to aesthetics than he cared to admit. Meanwhile, Georges Didi-Huberman argues that art historians have failed

to incorporate the "blow" that Freud's method dealt to the concept of representation. In his view, the dream-work's "means of representation" or "figuration" opens up, or indeed, *rends* the very logic of the image. Georges Didi-Huberman, *Confronting Images: Questioning the Ends of a Certain History of Art,* trans. John Goodman (University Park: Pennsylvania State University Press, 2005).

8. Virginia Woolf, *Thoughts on Peace in an Air Raid* (London: Penguin, 2009), 1.

9. Anzieu, *The Skin Ego.* See also Sara Flanders, introduction to *The Dream Discourse Today* (London: Routledge, 1993); and John A. Schneider, "From Freud's Dream-Work to Bion's Work of Dreaming: The Changing Conception of Dreaming in Psychoanalytic Theory," *International Journal of Psychoanalysis* 91 (2010): 521–40.

10. The concept is also discussed in "A Note on the 'Mystic Writing-Pad'" (1925), *SE,* 29:227–32.

11. Freud, *Moses and Monotheism* (1939), *SE,* 23:126. The optical metaphor is mentioned in *The Interpretation of Dreams, SE,* 5:536.

12. Sarah Kofman offers a fuller picture of Freud's use of the photographic metaphor in *Camera Obscura: Of Ideology,* trans. Will Straw (Ithaca, N.Y.: Cornell University Press, 1998). Ulrich Baer traces the connection between the experience of trauma and the photographic image further in *Spectral Evidence: The Photography of Trauma* (Cambridge, Mass.: MIT Press, 2002). In a less theoretical sense, however, the idea that photography provides a "protective shield" is plainly evident in the way any number of human rights organizations make the distribution of cameras central to their project of monitoring violent abuses. To cite just one example, in 2007 B'Tselem, the Israeli Information Center for Human Rights in the Occupied Territories, launched a camera distribution project, providing Palestinians living in high-conflict areas with video cameras, with the goal of bringing "the reality of their lives under occupation to the attention of the Israeli and international public, exposing and seeking redress for violations of human rights." See http://www.btselem.org.

13. Julia Kristeva, "Thinking about Liberty in Dark Times," in *Hatred and Forgiveness,* trans. Jeanine Herman (New York: Columbia University Press, 2010), 20.

14. In this respect Kristeva seems to depart from Freud's view in *Beyond the Pleasure Principle* that there is no such system of defense that protects against stimuli coming from the inside. Compellingly, if unelaborated here, Kristeva imagines literature provides "a refuge from our loves and insomnias, our states of grace and crisis" (ibid.).

15. According to a report by Stanford and New York Universities' law schools, the presence of armed drones, "terrorizes men, women, and children, giving rise to anxiety and psychological trauma among civilian communities. Those living under drones have to face the constant worry that a deadly strike may be fired at

any moment, and the knowledge that they are powerless to protect themselves." See International Human Rights and Conflict Resolution Clinic (Stanford Law School) and Global Justice Clinic (NYU School of Law), *Living under Drones: Death, Injury, and Trauma to Civilians from US Drone Practices in Pakistan* (September 2012), vii. http://living under drones.org.

16. One contemporary model of such civil defense is Abounaddara, an anonymous, self-taught filmmaking collective based in Syria that produces short documentary videos at a rate of one per week. At the time of writing, the collective has produced more than four hundred videos. In a concept paper, Abounaddara claims a "right to the image," which they define as a bundle of rights associated with the principle that every person is entitled to equal concern and respect in the design and structure of society. Their videos seek to counter the mainstream images of victims—"human debris"—with images of human persons struggling to live life with dignity and peace. See www.abounaddara.com. Researchers led by Eyal Weizman at Goldsmiths have also developed a series of multimedia tools for journalists, researchers, human rights monitors, and citizens in a digital age to map complex events, such as conflicts, protests, or crises, as they develop. See http://www.gold.ac.uk/news/pattrn.

17. See Pablo Picasso, *Paintings, Watercolors, Drawings and Sculpture: A Comprehensive Illustrated Catalogue,* vol. 6, *Spanish Civil War, 1937–1939* (San Francisco: Alan Wofsy Fine Arts, 1995), xi; and Ian Patterson, *Guernica and Total War* (Cambridge, Mass.: Harvard University Press, 2007).

18. Virginia Woolf, "Three Guineas" (1938), in *A Room of One's Own and Three Guineas* (London: Penguin Books, 2000), 125.

19. It would not take long for the bombs to reach Woolf in London. In "Thoughts on Peace in an Air Raid," written shortly before her suicide in the spring of 1941, she describes "the queer experience" of "lying in the dark and listening to the zoom of a hornet, which may at any moment sting you to death. It is a sound that interrupts cool and consecutive thinking about peace. Yet it is a sound—far more than prayers and anthems—that should compel one to think about peace." Woolf, *Thoughts on Peace in an Air Raid,* 1. The short piece is an exemplar of the way the "work" of writing can help to dispel the destructive force, even as it betrays something of the difficulty of the struggle to maintain a protective shield for the mind in such times.

20. Jacques Rancière, *The Emancipated Spectator* (New York: Verso, 2009).

21. Ernestine Carter, ed., *Bloody but Unbowed: Pictures of Britain under Fire* (London: Lund Humphries; New York: Scribners, 1941), n.p.

22. Ibid., n.p.

23. Freud, "Humour" (1927), *SE,* 21:161.

24. Antony Penrose, *The Lives of Lee Miller* (London: Thames and Hudson, 1985), 103.

25. Of course there was civil resistance among the occupied countries. Lee Miller's lover, Roland Penrose, made a clandestine trip into occupied France to compile documents made by the intellectuals of the French Resistance, publishing a collection, titled *In the Service of the People,* in 1945. In chapter 2, "The Crime against the Spirit," he writes of the Nazi occupation: "Not only was the repression exercised by them political but it also attacked liberty of thought and expression. It meant the reversal of long standing rights and fundamental ideas. In the [Nazi] campaign for re-education, the national inscriptions dating from the French revolution such as 'Liberty, Equality, Brotherhood' were erased from public buildings and from the coinage. . . . Life without their habitual liberties was inconceivable. . . . No matter who they were, young or old, peasants or cultured Parisians, this alone was enough to awaken revolt." See Roland Penrose, *In the Service of the People* (London: William Heinemann, 1945), 8.

26. Walter Benjamin, "The Work of Age in the Age of Mechanical Reproducibility" (1936), in *Selected Writings,* vol. 3, *1935–1938,* 101–33.

27. Freud, *New Introductory Lectures* (1932), SE, 22:7.

28. Freud, *Beyond the Pleasure Principle,* 32. For discussion of this transition see Joshua Levy, "The Dream in *Beyond the Pleasure Principle* and Beyond," in *On Freud's "Beyond the Pleasure Principle,"* ed. Salman Akhtar and Mary K. O'Neil (London: Karnac, 2011), 128–53.

29. Sándor Ferenczi, "On the Revision of *The Interpretation of Dreams*" (1931), in *Final Contributions to the Problems and Methods of Psychoanalysis* (London: Hogarth Press, 1955), 238.

30. Freud, *New Introductory Lectures* (1932), SE, 22:27–30.

31. Wilfred Bion, *War Memoirs, 1917–1919,* ed. Francesca Bion (London: Karnac, 1997), 25 and 94.

32. Ibid., 94.

33. Wilfred Bion, *A Memoir of the Future* (London: Karnac, 1991), 239.

34. Bion, *Learning from Experience,* 15.

35. In *Beyond the Pleasure Principle,* Freud assigns the protective function to the perceptual consciousness (*Pcpt.-Cs.*) system, which "must lie on the borderline between inside and outside; it must be turned towards the external world and must envelop the other psychical systems" (24). As he later notes, *protection against* stimuli is, in fact, a more important function for the living organism than *reception of* stimuli, and the common traumatic neurosis is the consequence of a breach of the protective shield (31). One of Bion's points of emphasis was that dream-work can get damaged, and when it does, our capacity to digest and process emotional experience is hindered. See Michael Eigen, "Damaged Dream-Work," in *Damaged Bonds* (London: Karnac, 2001), 43–61.

36. Anzieu, *The Skin Ego,* 211.

37. Ibid., 214–15.

38. Caitlin Davis suggests Miller was not permitted to photograph the dead during the Blitz. But after D-Day, Miller gained U.S. Army accreditation and headed to the European front. She traveled with the units that liberated Buchenwald and then Dachau concentration camps, and there she did indeed train her camera on the dead, managing to transform even this difficult "raw matter" into remarkably potent signs. See Davis, "Lee Miller's Revenge on Culture: Photojournalism, Surrealism, and Autobiography," *Women's Art Journal* 27, no. 1 (Spring–Summer 2006): 3–9; and Sharon Sliwinski, "Visual Testimony: Lee Miller's Dachau," *Journal of Visual Culture* 9, no. 3 (December 2010): 389–408.

39. Miller's contact sheets are housed at the Lee Miller Archives, Blitz folder, Farley Farm House, East Sussex, England. http://www.leemiller.co.uk.

40. André Breton introduced "compulsive beauty" (as a cognate of the marvelous) in *Nadja* (1928) and later developed the concept in *L'amour fou* (1937). Surrealism was for a long time seen, as Breton wanted it to be seen, as a movement of love and liberation. But as Hal Foster has argued, surrealism was in fact born out of the traumas of the First World War and is best described as an art given over to the uncanny, the compulsion to repeat, and the death drive. See Foster, *Compulsive Beauty* (Cambridge, Mass.: MIT, 1993).

5. The Colonial Defense

1. Frantz Fanon, *The Wretched of the Earth,* trans. Richard Philcox (New York: Grove Press, 2004), 44. For an account of this book's being seized by police, see David Macey, *Frantz Fanon: A Biography* (London: Verso, 2000), xii. The reception of Fanon's work in France undoubtedly fell within the larger cultural and political taboo surrounding the Algerian War. The very term *guerre d'Algérie* was publicly forbidden in France until 1999, when the National Assembly passed a law allowing the use of the term.

2. My account is largely culled from Homi Bhabha's foreword to the new edition of *The Wretched of the Earth*, "Framing Fanon," xxviii–xxix.

3. Hannah Arendt, *On Violence* (New York: Harcourt Brace, 1970), 4.

4. Ibid., 22 and 11.

5. Albert Memmi, "The Impossible Life of Frantz Fanon," *Massachusetts Review* 14, no. 1 (Winter 1973): 11, 25, and 18.

6. Henry Louis Gates Jr., "Critical Fanonisms," *Critical Inquiry* 17 (Spring 1991): 458.

7. Kobena Mercer, Stuart Hall, and others have noted that early generations of readers privileged the Marxist themes of Fanon's later work, while the identity wars of the 1980s provided a backdrop for a renewed interest in Fanon's first and most explicitly psychoanalytic text, *Black Skin, White Masks,* trans. Charles Lam Markmann (London: Pluto Press, 2008). See Kobena Mercer, "Busy in the Ruins

of the Wretched Phantasia," in *Mirage: Enigmas of Race and Desire* (London: Institute of Contemporary Arts/International Institute of International Visual Arts, 1994), and Stuart Hall, "The After-Life of Frantz Fanon: Why Fanon? Why Now? Why *Black Skin, White Masks*?," in *The Fact of Blackness: Frantz Fanon and Visual Representation*, ed. Alan Read (Seattle: Bay Press, 1996), 12–37.

8. Fanon, *Black Skin, White Masks*, 7.

9. Fanon, *The Wretched of the Earth*, 183.

10. Alice Cherki, *Frantz Fanon: A Portrait*, trans. Nadia Benabid (Ithaca, N.Y.: Cornell University Press, 2006), 2. Cherki worked with Fanon in Blida and has subsequently studied his unpublished psychiatric writings and the entirety of his case notes on two talking cures that Fanon conducted in 1959 and 1960.

11. Fanon was not entirely silent on the question of subaltern women. Although he once provocatively declared that he knew "nothing" of the woman of color, he devoted a chapter to an analysis of Mayotte Capécia's *Je suis Martiniquaise* (I am a Martinican woman); see *Black Skin, White Masks*, 138. And in "Algeria Unveiled," Fanon surveyed the mutable and contradictory cultural meanings attributed to Algerian women's dress, and more specifically what he calls the "historic dynamism of the veil." Fanon claims that the veil functions, for the European, as a fetish, signaling colonialism's highly sexualized economy of the gaze. See Frantz Fanon, *A Dying Colonialism* (New York: Grove Press, 1967), 35–63. This analysis of the veil does not, of course, amount to a direct engagement with subaltern women's own discourse. As Diana Fuss (among others) has shown, Fanon's analysis of colonial mimesis repeatedly runs aground on the question of sexual difference. See Fuss, *Identification Papers* (New York: Routledge, 1995), 141–65.

12. Simone de Beauvoir and Gisèle Halimi, *Djamila Boupacha: The Story of a Young Algerian Girl Which Shocked Liberal French Opinion*, trans. Peter Green (New York: Macmillan, 1962), 194. Boupacha was an FLN militant who was arrested in 1960 for allegedly planning to bomb a café in Algiers. During her interrogation she was tortured and raped. With the help of Gisèle Halimi and Simone de Beauvoir, she brought a suit against her torturers. The case is often credited with changing public opinion about the methods used by the French army in Algeria.

13. Spivak is actually borrowing and adapting Pierre Macherey's phrase. Gayatri Chakravorty Spivak, "Can the Subaltern Speak?," in *Marxism and the Interpretation of Culture*, ed. Cary Nelson and Lawrence Grossberg (Urbana: University of Illinois Press, 1988), 286.

14. I am thinking of Toni Morrison's *Beloved* in particular, which is based on the historical case of Margaret Garner, who murdered one of her children when her slave owner recaptured the family. My thinking here is indebted to Mark Reinhardt's *Who Speaks for Margaret Garner?* (Minneapolis: University of Minnesota Press, 2010).

15. Macey, *Frantz Fanon*, 91.

16. Fanon, *Black Skin, White Masks*, 121. In his discussion of this passage, Lewis R. Gordon emphasizes that the French word *nègre* can mean "Negro" or "nigger" depending on context. See Gordon, *What Fanon Said: A Philosophical Introduction to His Life and Thought* (New York: Fordham University Press, 2015), 22.

17. Fanon, *Black Skin, White Masks*, 84.

18. The original title of Fanon's fifth chapter is *"L'expérience vécue de l'homme noir,"* which has been persistently translated—some would say *mis*translated— into English as "The Fact of Blackness." This translation manages to obliterate the phenomenological frame of reference and even reverse the terms of the author's argument. Fanon had attended Merleau-Ponty's lectures while he was a student in Lyon; *l'expérience vécue* was the philosopher's translation of the widely used German term *Erlebnis*. On one level, Fanon's book can be read as a complex quarrel with Merleau-Ponty's account of embodied experience and its relationship to freedom. See Ronald A. T. Judy, "Fanon's Black Body of Experience," in *Fanon: A Critical Reader*, ed. Lewis R. Gordon et al. (London: Blackwell: 1996), 53–73, and Jeremy Weate, "Fanon, Merleau-Ponty, and the Difference of Phenomenology," in *Race*, ed. Robert Bernasconi (Oxford: Blackwell, 2000), 169–83.

19. Maurice Merleau-Ponty, *Phenomenology of Perception*, trans. Colin Smith (New York: Routledge, 1962), 146.

20. Fanon, *Black Skin, White Masks*, 84.

21. Ibid., 4.

22. Ibid., 75.

23. Elizabeth Roudinesco, *Jacques Lacan and Co.: A History of Psychoanalysis in France, 1925–1985*, trans. Jeffery Mehlman (Chicago: University of Chicago Press, 1990), 234.

24. Maurice Bloch, foreword to Mannoni's *Prospero and Caliban: The Psychology of Colonization*, trans. Pamela Powesland (Ann Arbor: University of Michigan Press, 1990), 8–9.

25. See Macey, *Frantz Fanon*, 186–88; and also Philip Leymarie, "Painful Memories of the Revolt of 1947: Deafening Silence on a Horrifying Repression," *Le Monde Diplomatique*, http://mondediplo.com/1997/03/02madagascar.

26. Mannoni offers only two short, impressionistic accounts of the massacres in his text; Mannoni, *Prospero and Caliban*, 76–79 and 87–88. There has been considerable discussion of the debate between Fanon and Mannoni, much of which has been summarized by Christopher Lane, "Psychoanalysis and Colonialism Redux: Why Mannoni's 'Prospero Complex' Still Haunts Us," *Journal of Modern Literature* 25, no. 3/4 (Summer 2002): 127–49.

27. Mannoni, *Prospero and Caliban*, 89; Frantz Fanon, *Black Skin, White Masks*, 61.

28. Mannoni, *Prospero and Caliban*, 89.

29. Mannoni does not say more about this context, but adds that he has dismissed those examples that appeared to be inventions: "not because such fantasies are without interest but because their interpretation is more difficult. By contrast with the real dreams they were all very 'optimistic.'" In the "real" dreams, in other words, the terror is undisguised. Mannoni, *Prospero and Caliban,* 91 n. 2.

30. Ibid., 90–91; emphasis in original.

31. Fanon, *Black Skin, White Masks,* 77–78; emphasis in original.

32. Ibid., 79.

33. Hanna Segal, "On Symbolism," (1978), reprinted in *Psychoanalysis, Literature, and War: Papers 1972–1995,* ed. John Steiner (London: Routledge, 1997); and George Devereux, *Reality and Dream: Psychotherapy of a Plains Indian* (New York: International University Press, 1951).

34. Macey, *Frantz Fanon,* 217–38.

35. Fanon, *The Wretched of the Earth,* 181.

36. What Fanon meant in his call for "violence" is far from settled. His interlocutors—Sartre and Arendt representative among them—did not use this word to mean the same things. Sartre celebrated the FLN's violent revolt as synonymous with freedom; Arendt regarded it as the death of politics. According to Homi Bhabha, Fanon took neither view. He held out hope that the Algerian people's struggle for liberation would result in a new kind of humanism, and he agreed with the FLN that violent resistance had become a necessary part of this social transformation. See Bhabha, "Framing Fanon," xxxvi.

37. Fanon, *The Wretched of the Earth,* 183.

38. "Our purpose, in any case, is to demonstrate that any torture deeply *dislocates,* as might be expected, the personality of the tortured." Ibid., 183 n. 22.

39. See Jean Laplanche and J.-B. Pontalis's entry in *The Language of Psychoanalysis,* trans. Donald Nicholson-Smith (New York: W. W. Norton, 1973), 121–24.

40. Peter B. Neubauer, "The Role of Displacement in Psychoanalysis," *Psychoanalytic Study of the Child* 49 (1994): 107–19.

41. Freud, "On Dreams," 655.

42. Anna Freud, *The Analysis of Defense: The Ego and the Mechanisms of Defense Revisited,* with Joseph Sandler (New York: International Universities Press, 1985).

43. Fanon, *The Wretched of the Earth,* 217.

44. Ibid., 193.

45. Ibid., 199–201.

46. Ibid., 199.

47. As Diana Fuss puts it, "The daily translations of Arabic and Kabyle into French could not avoid reproducing, within the space of the clinical treatment, the very structure of the colonial relations." Moreover, what is lost in this translation is the "speaking unconscious . . . the slips and reversals, the substitutions and

mispronunciations . . . that provide the analyst with his most important interpretative material." Fuss, *Identification Papers*, 162.

48. Fanon, *The Wretched of the Earth*, 187–88. Fanon's original French passage about the dream reads: "*Cependant, plusieurs entretiens et un rêve (le malade assiste à la rapide putréfaction d'un petit chat avec dégagement d'odeurs insupportables) nous conduisent dans une tout autre direction. 'Cette fille, nous dit-il un jour (il s'agit de sa petite fille), a quelque chose de pourri en elle' *" ([Paris: Éditions La Découverte/ Poche, 2002], 243).

49. Fanon, *The Wretched of the Earth*, 188–89. Last emphasis added.

50. Michael Eigan, *Damaged Bonds*.

51. Gayatri Chakravorty Spivak, "Can the Subaltern Speak?," in *Can the Subaltern Speak? Reflections on the History of an Idea*, ed. Rosalind C. Morris (New York: Columbia University Press, 2010), 21.

52. Ibid., 22.

53. The French is on page 243 of the book published in 2002 by Éditions La Découverte/Poche; Philcox's translation appears on page 188 of the 2004 Grove English-language edition; Constance Farrington's rendering is on page 257 of the 1963 Grove version.

54. See Debra B. Bergoffen, *Contesting the Forms of Genocidal Rape: Affirming the Dignity of the Vulnerable Body* (New York: Routledge, 2012); Marnia Lazreg, *Torture and the Twilight of Empire: From Algiers to Baghdad* (Princeton, N.J.: Princeton University Press, 2008).

55. Anne Carson, "Variations on the Right to Remain Silent," in *Nay, Rather* (London: Center for Writers and Translators of the American University of Paris/ Sylph Editions, 2013), 4.

56. Julia Kristeva, *Intimate Revolt: The Powers and Limits of Psychoanalysis*, vol. 2, trans. Jeanine Herman (New York: Columbia University Press, 2002).

6. On Folding Force

1. Charlotte Beradt, "Dreams under Dictatorship," *Free World*, October 1943, 333–37.

2. Beradt begins her book-length study with this dream. Charlotte Beradt, *The Third Reich of Dreams*, trans. Adriane Gottwald (Chicago: Quadrangle Books, 1968), 5.

3. Ibid.

4. Ibid., 7–8.

5. Ibid., 9.

6. Beradt, "Dreams under Dictatorship," 333. The journalist took the precaution of camouflaging her notes. The Nazi Party was given the code name "the family," and Hitler, Göring, and Goebbels became "Uncle Hans," "Uncle Gustav,"

and "Uncle Gerhard," respectively. Beradt hid these odd "family anecdotes" in the pages of her books and eventually began sending them out in letters to addresses abroad.

7. Reinhart Koselleck, "Terror and Dream: Methodological Remarks on the Experience of Time during the Third Reich," in *Futures Past: On the Semantics of Historical Time*, trans. Keith Tribe (New York: Columbia University Press, 2004), 217. Koselleck deemed dreams "a first-rate" historical source that is indispensable to research into the history of the everyday (330). Peter Bourke also addresses the significance of dream for cultural history in *Varieties of Cultural History* (Ithaca, N.Y.: Cornell University Press, 1997).

8. Although anxiety dreams are far more common in Beradt's study, she does include several examples of wish dreams, noting that these dreams "express people's natural longing for equality and recognition, their yearning for things lost." However, even wish dreams seem to offer evidence of "how the wounds inflicted by dictatorship bleed and hurt, even though they are not bodily injuries." Beradt, "Dreams under Dictatorship," 336–37.

9. Ibid., 337.

10. Beradt, *The Third Reich of Dreams*, 21.

11. Ibid., 9.

12. After the Second World War, the question of how to traverse a violent political history saw vigorous debate. In 1952, Theodor Adorno participated in a group experiment, revealing residual National Socialist attitudes among the recently democratized Germans. In the title of his 1959 radio address, Adorno used the German phrase *Aufarbeitung* ("working through") in deliberate contrast to the term that was being mobilized in postwar Germany at the time, *Vergangenheitsbewältigung*. This latter term connotes a confrontation with the past, but also implies a sense of overcoming (*Vergangenheit* = past; *Bewältigung* = coming to terms with, mastering, wrestling into submission). Adorno was vigorously opposed to the idea that the history of National Socialism could somehow be wrestled into submission. Theodor Adorno, "The Meaning of Working through the Past," reprinted in *Can One Live after Auschwitz? A Philosophical Reader*, ed. Rolf Tiedemann, trans. Harry W. Pickford (Stanford, Calif.: Stanford University Press, 2003), 3–18. Daniel Pick leads a research group at Birkbeck exploring the history of the human sciences and "psy" professions during the Cold War in a project titled "Hidden Persuaders: Brainwashing, Culture, Clinical Knowledge and the Cold War Human Sciences, c. 1950–1990," http://www.bbk.ac.uk/hiddenpersuaders.

13. Charlotte Beradt cites this statement as an epigraph to the first chapter of *The Third Reich of Dreams*, 3.

14. In the first preface to *The Interpretation of Dreams*, Freud asks his readers to grant him "the right to the freedom of thought—in my dream-life, if nowhere else." Freud, *SE*, 4:xxiii–xxiv.

15. Michel Foucault, "The Subject and Power" (1982), in *Power: Essential Works of Michel Foucault*, vol. 3, *1954–1984*, ed. James D. Faubion (New York: New Press, 2001), 328.

16. Ibid., 342.

17. Foucault, *The Care of the Self*, 1–36. Foucault also elaborates on these practices as a form of ethics in an interview, "The Ethics of the Concern for Self as a Practice of Freedom." Gilles Deleuze describes these practices as "foldings" in his mediation on Foucault's work: *Foucault*, trans. Séan Hand (New York: Bloomsbury, 2006).

18. Beginning in the fall of 1980, Foucault began delivering a number of lectures and seminars that sought to trace the history of these critical techniques of self-formation, which he named "techniques of self." Transcripts of several of these lectures and seminars have been published; see, for instance: Michel Foucault, "About the Beginning of the Hermeneutics of the Self: Two Lectures at Dartmouth," *Political Theory* 21, no. 2 (May 1993): 198–227; "Technologies of the Self," in *Technologies of the Self: A Seminar with Michel Foucault*, ed. Luther H. Martin, Huck Gutman, Patrick H. Hutton (Amherst: University of Massachusetts Press, 1988), 16–49; *Wrong-doing, Truth-telling: The Function of Avowal in Justice*, ed. Fabienne Brion and Bernard E. Harcourt, trans. Stephen W. Sawyer, (Chicago: University of Chicago Press, 2014).

19. See Sharpe, *Dream Analysis*, 1–39, and Jacques Lacan, "The Signification of the Phallus" (1959) in *Écrits*, 575–84. Sharpe explored a wide range of poetic devices, while Lacan privileged metaphor and metonymy. Lacan also provocatively claimed that the unconscious laws that governed the human being are, in fact, linguistic rules. I suspect Sharpe would have taken the opposite position, that is, that linguistic rules reflect the structures of the unconscious.

20. Freud probably has Galton's well-known attempts to visualize "the Jewish type" in mind, since the dream in question dealt with his own racial anxieties. See Freud, *The Interpretation of Dreams* (1900), *SE*, 4:293. Freud also mentions photographic composites in relation to the dream-work in lecture 11 of his *Introductory Lectures on Psychoanalysis* (1916–17), *SE*, 15:171–72. Galton described his experimental process in (among other places) an article titled "Photographic Composites," *Journal of the Anthropological Institute of Britain and Ireland* 8 (1879): 132–44. Carol Zemel discusses the racial anxieties contained in Freud's dream in *Looking Jewish: Visual Culture and Modern Diaspora* (Bloomington: Indiana University Press, 2015), and Jonathan Fardy pursues the significance of Freud's photographic metaphor in "'To Adopt': Freud, Photography, and the Optical Unconscious," in *Photography and the Optical Unconscious*, ed. Shawn Michelle Smith and Sharon Sliwinski (Durham, N.C.: Duke University Press, 2017).

21. Christopher Phillips, introduction to Matthew Teitelbaum, ed., *Montage and Modern Life: 1919–1942* (Cambridge, Mass.: MIT Press, 1992), 22.

22. The slogan appears in Heartfield's first photomontage for *AIZ*, a self-portrait in which he beheads the Berlin chief of police with a pair of scissors. For broader discussions of Heartfield's work see Sabine Kriebel, "Manufacturing Discontent: John Heartfield's Mass Medium," *New German Critique*, no. 107 (2009): 53–88, and Andrés Mario Zervigón, *John Heartfield and the Agitated Image: Photography, Persuasion, and the Rise of Avant-Garde Photomontage* (Chicago: University of Chicago Press, 2012).

23. Reinhart Koselleck emphasizes this point in his afterword to Beradt's *The Third Reich of Dreams*, republished in English in *The Practice of Conceptual History: Timing History, Spacing Concepts*, trans. Todd Presner (Stanford, Calif.: Stanford University Press, 2002), 335.

24. The notion of work—*Arbeit* in German—drives Freud's model of the psychical apparatus. The agency known as the unconscious is constantly at work, and the operations of the dream-work preside over this unconscious economy, which is to say, the laws that govern dream-life also govern the workings of unconscious writ large. Correspondingly, one can find the idea of work underpinning many key psychoanalytic concepts. Apart from the dream-work, Freud used the term to describe humor (*Witzarbeit*) and the labor of mourning (*Trauerarbeit*), as well as any variety of related psychological processes that could all go under the heading "working out" (*Verbindung, Bearbeitung, Ausarbeitung, Aufarbeitung*). Among these various types of psychological work, dream-work is king. Freud leaned upon the specific operations of dream-work as he developed his unorthodox method of treatment; the work of dreaming provided Freud with a model for his "talking cure," or what he later defined as "working through" (*Durcharbeitung*). Subsequent clinicians have elaborated and expanded upon this view, effectively treating the consulting room as a space to help strengthen the patient's capacity to dream: supporting the patient's capacity to represent and transform—to *transvalue*—the meaning of past and present emotional situations and fantasies. Ella Freeman Sharpe was among the first to emphasize the significance of dream within the psychoanalytic task. In a series of lectures delivered to the British Psycho-Analytical Society in the 1930s, she argued that dream analysis helped the patient "tolerate and deal with instinctual impulses in a rational and effective way within a socialized community," but even more evocatively, that careful consideration of dream-life could produce a "revelation of the unknown, implicit in the known." Sharpe, *Dream Analysis*, 17–18. The relationship between dreaming and analytic technique has been richly developed and elaborated in the clinical literature. See, for instance, Segal, "The Function of Dreams"; Bion, *Learning from Experience*; Donald Meltzer, *Dream-life: A Re-examination of the Psycho-analytical Theory and Technique* (Oxford: Clunie Press, 1984); J.-B. Pontalis, *Frontiers in Psychoanalysis*; Thomas Ogden, *This Art of Psychoanalysis: Dreaming Undreamt Dreams and Interrupted Cries* (London: Karnac, 2005); Antonio Ferro, "Transformations in Dreaming and Characters in

the Psychoanalytic Field," *International Journal of Psychoanalysis* 90 (2009): 209–30; and Christopher Bollas, "The Wisdom of the Dream," *The Christopher Bollas Reader* (London: Routledge, 2011), 249–58. For an excellent overview, see Sara Flanders's introduction to *The Dream Discourse Today*. Mai Wegener has also pursued some of the tensions in Freud's use of the term "work" in "Why Should Dreaming Be a Form of Work? On Work, Economy, and Enjoyment," in *Jacques Lacan: Between Psychoanalysis and Politics,* ed. Samo Tomšič and Andreja Zevnik (London: Routledge, 2016), 164–80.

25. Sarah Kofman, *Smothered Words,* trans. Madeline Dobie (Evanston, Ill.: Northwestern University Press, 1997), 9–10.

26. Sarah Kofman, *Rue Ordener, Rue Labat,* trans. Ann Smock (Lincoln: University of Nebraska Press, 1996), 10.

27. Kofman, *Smothered Words,* 9–10.

28. Kofman, *Rue Ordener, Rue Labat,* 12.

29. Toni Morrison, "Unspeakable Things Unspoken: The Afro-American Presence in American Literature," Tanner Lecture on Human Values, delivered at the University of Michigan, October 7, 1998. Available online http://tannerlectures .utah.edu/_documents/a-to-z/m/morrison90.pdf.

30. Kofman, *Rue Ordener, Rue Labat,* 11.

31. Ibid.

Index